The 20 British Prime Ministers
of the 20th century

Baldwin

ANNE PERKINS

HAUS PUBLISHING · LONDON

First published in Great Britain in 2006 by
Haus Publishing Limited
26 Cadogan Court
Draycott Avenue
London SW3 3BX

www.hauspublishing.co.uk

A CIP catalogue record for this book is available from the British Library

ISBN 1-904950-60-4

Designed by BrillDesign
Typeset in Garamond 3 by MacGuru Ltd
info@macguru.org.uk

Printed and bound by Graphicom, Vicenza

Front cover: John Holder

Contents

Part One: THE LIFE
Chapter 1: Origins   1
Chapter 2: If you can wait ... (1922–4)   16

Part Two: THE LEADERSHIP
Chapter 3: If you can dream ... (1923–4)   31
Chapter 4: Triumph (1924–6)   47
Chapter 5: Disaster (1926–31)   62
Chapter 6: Worn-out Tools (1931–7)   76
Chapter 7: Nerve and Sinew (1931–7)   90
Chapter 8: Or walk with Kings:
            The Abdication Crisis 1936   110

Part Three: THE LEGACY
Chapter 9: The Baldwin Era   125

Notes   142
Chronology   149
Further Reading   160
Picture Sources   164
Index   166

Part One

THE LIFE

Chapter 1: Origins

I was born in the year which saw the publication of Marx's Capital [sic] ... and Disraeli's extension of the franchise to working men ... I mention these two events ... because they are the keys to much of what has happened in the past seventy years ...[1]

It is a curious fact that, at least for a time, Stanley Baldwin gave his name to the period between the end of the First World War and the start of the Second. The 'Baldwin Era', the decades of the Charleston and the slump, of upper-class frivolity and working-class penury, political instability and the ascendancy of the dictators, are strange years to bear the name of a politician whose beliefs were shaped in the reign of Queen Victoria. Baldwin, like most of his colleagues in government, had been brought up in a world quite differently ordered. The Great War had shaken that order to its core. Its survivors, men too old to fight, felt most profoundly that they were in power because the generation that might have succeeded them had died among the barbed wire, the bullets and the shells of the first global conflict. To their years in government in the 1920s and 1930s, to the Brave New World, they brought the pessimism of a generation that had seen its own assumptions destroyed, who now felt threatened by change, by the triumph of materialism over spirituality, of the masses over the individual.

Baldwin's *annus mirabilis*, the year of *Das Kapital* and Disraeli's Reform Act, was 1867. He was the first and only child of a prosperous ironmaster, Alfred Baldwin, and his wife Louisa MacDonald, of Bewdley in Worcestershire. From Louisa, he inherited a Celtic streak along with sandy-coloured hair and blue eyes; from his father, a growing business and a sense of service; from his birthplace, a sense of Englishness. Baldwin never lived more than ten miles from Bewdley. The Malvern Hills were the backdrop to his private life and often a prop to his public image as a countryman, a man who would rather keep pigs than trouble with politics.

In the Baldwin family, pigs were a lifelong private joke. As a small boy, his parents made him a present of a toy pig. Thereafter, family and friends added to his collection. Rudyard Kipling, Baldwin's first cousin, wrote him a poem that began: 'Some to Women, some to Wine – /Some to Wealth or Power incline,/ Proper people cherish Swine.'[2] Kipling presented it to Baldwin in 1919, inscribed on the flank of a wooden pig made by a war veteran.

As a child, most of his waking hours were spent not in the farmyard or in the countryside, but in the immediate neighbourhood of heavy industry. When he was still an infant, his father bought out one part of the Baldwin family's industrial holdings and became sole proprietor of the sheet-metal firm of E P & W Baldwin. The family moved a few miles from Bewdley to Wilden, just north of Stourport, where they lived in the ironmaster's house in a village that was dominated by 'the works'. The relationship between master and men, benevolently paternalistic, was not unusual for the time although in Baldwin's later campaigns against the politics of class, it became a kind of industrial utopia where the obligations of status of both master and men contributed to a wholesome, harmonious existence. A fête to which the entire village was invited marked the young Baldwin's birthdays, a public function with bands and balloons and sack races, a great community event. The child at the centre of it became a prince, touched by the burdens of the patriarch.

Although he spent much of the first 21 years of his life away from home at school and university, this patch of Worcestershire retained an unshakeable hold on his affections and gave distinctive colouring to his political imagination. His literary mother and his bookish father encouraged his romantic spirit. There was an extensive library at Wilden and in the holidays stimulating visits to his artistic extended family. All politicians' outlooks are shaped by their own experience, but Baldwin, despite later travels throughout Europe and in America, seems to have relied with extraordinary consistency and confidence on what he learned from contacts made at work, at church and in the local politics of this small semi-rural world. Years later, in passages of some of his most famous speeches, a nostalgia for the sights and sounds of childhood was transposed into evocative motifs of a semi-mythical world: the ploughman, a particular birdsong (sometimes the lark, usually the distinctive rasp of the corncrake) and the flap and caw of rooks coming home to roost. In adulthood, Baldwin's favourite writer was Mary Webb, author of a series of mystical depictions of Shropshire country folk which appealed to his own idealised vision of rural life. As a child, he read precociously from the Victorian classics, especially Sir Walter Scott. Various cousins were frequent companions: two of his mother Louisa's sisters had married into artistic circles, one to the neo-classical painter, Sir Edward Poynter and another to the pre-Raphaelite, Sir Edward Burne Jones.

A third sister married John Lockwood Kipling. While they were in India, their son, Rudyard, a couple of years older than Stanley, had been sent home to school in England. Another cousin, Harold Baldwin, perhaps his closest friend, lived at Wilden after his own father died. It was a source of great grief when as an undergraduate he developed epilepsy and had to live as a semi-invalid.

Literature and the arts, in their more comfortable and less provocative forms, were one enduring interest. (Years later, he shuddered with ill-concealed horror when he unveiled Epstein's *Rima* in Kensington Gardens.) A concern for the spiritual was another. Both his parents, brought up in devoutly Methodist families that had produced ministers and missionaries in the recent past, had converted to a high form of Anglicanism. They built a church and a church school in Wilden; their lives were imbued with notions of Christian social concern, a sense of responsibility not for changing the lives of their workers but for ensuring that they were in neither spiritual nor material want. In twenty years in business, Stanley was to boast in his maiden speech in the House of Commons, *there had never been the shadow of a dispute with any of his own men.*[3] His understanding of the demands of industry and his familiarity with the outlook of the working man influenced his later ideas about what it meant to be a Conservative in the first part of the 20th century.

The emphasis on service in the ethical and moral framework that Baldwin took from his family, together with a strong faith, led him briefly to consider a career in the Church. He left nothing to explain why he preferred public life instead. But a sense of religious purpose underlay his decision to enter politics, although he made little public show of it. He might write to his mother: *We both believe there is guidance in these things. I never sought a place, never expected it, and suddenly a way opened and an offer of wider service was made. If one tackles public life in the right spirit, it is unselfish service,*[4] but there was never a show of church-going. Nor did he speak directly of the importance of his Christian convictions, from which he learned always to take the harder path. Instead, he intended his Christianity to be in everything he did.

Louisa and Alfred were distant but influential figures in the young Stanley's life. Louisa wrote novels and often was reduced by an unspecified complaint to lying in darkened rooms. The handsomely bewhiskered Alfred dominates contemporary photographs with a sharpness of gaze that betrays the successful businessman. Stanley's education reflected his family's growing social status: with his cousin Ambrose Poynter, he went at the age of ten to a prep school, Hawtrey's, with a view to continuing on to Eton. Instead he was separated from Ambrose, whom he was considered to dominate, and went to the rival school, Harrow, where his academic career, initially promising, declined

> *We do not think of the laws of gravitation when we move our limbs,* Baldwin said in a 1931 address on religion and national life, *We need not proclaim our religious convictions at every street corner. What matters is that religion should sway our motives, sustain our principles, surround and bathe our spirits like a secret atmosphere as we go about our work.*[5]

sharply. Presumably echoing a story first told to his official biographer G M Young,[6] subsequent biographers cite a discipline problem involving a pornographic joke which, if true, must be the only recorded occasion when Baldwin acted with less than propriety. He went up to Cambridge and, he confessed later, was overcome with an indolence that resulted in a third class degree. It has been said that this was a disappointment to his parents. Yet most history graduates at the time were awarded third class degrees, and there is no contemporary evidence of his father's chagrin apart from a quote from Baldwin himself, drily remembered many years later when he was an acclaimed politician. 'I hope you don't get a third in life.'

After Cambridge, Baldwin settled into the conventions of life in the late Victorian upper-middle classes, a kind of Forsytean progression where an increasingly successful family business absorbed his working hours, public works his evenings, and family parties the weekends. In 1898 he oversaw the business's flotation on the Stock Market, and in 1902 the rationalisation of its various arms which now stretched down into South Wales and across into the Black Country. A series of horizontal and vertical mergers brought the whole iron-working process, from commodity extraction to finishing, under one umbrella, partly in the hope of ensuring regular work for employees who now numbered in the thousands. E P & W Baldwin had a publicly-quoted value of £1 million (about £60 million at today's prices) which probably put it among the hundred largest British companies.[7]

In 1892 Alfred Baldwin was elected Conservative MP for Bewdley. The Baldwin family had once been Liberals, but at about the same time that they shed their Methodism, their political allegiance shifted too, a reaction to Gladstone's increasingly radical stance. For the next 16 years Alfred played a respected role as a Tory back-bencher. In the same year, Stanley, usually stricken with shyness among women, met and married the jolly, loyal, sporting Lucy Ridsdale, whom he was said to have first seen as she scored a half-century in a local cricket match. Lucy – Cissie to her family – was a friend of the Burne-Jones cousins who lived at Rotting-dean in Sussex. After the tragedy of a stillborn son in 1894, six healthy children followed, two sons and four daughters. Baldwin's family life remained deeply private, even after the election as a Labour MP in 1929 of his elder son Oliver, who was as openly homosexual as it was possible to be in an era of sexual prohibition (he lived with his partner, John Boyce, whom the Baldwins came to treat as part of the family). Lucy seems to have been tireless and inventive, filling the large Jacobean house at Astley, to which the family moved in 1902, with an Edwardian parade of large informal parties, tennis and cricket and, when he was at home, billiards with Stanley. She was more reluctant to accompany her husband on the long walks which he took almost as a daily routine whether he was in London or in the country. For companions on these excursions, she would summon friends, apparently untouched by jealousy of the close relationships which were formed with at least two companions – Phyllis Broome and later, and for 40 years or more, Joan 'Mimi' Davidson.

Financially secure, with a growing family and with a standing in local society reinforced by his role as parish councillor, county councillor, JP, school governor, a member of various friendly societies and the local Conservative Association, by 1904 Baldwin's thoughts had turned to following his father to Westminster. Even at school, parliament had been his intended destination. Disraeli, branches of whose Primrose league Baldwin nurtured at home in Worcestershire, was the prime minister of his formative years, he studied his speeches at Harrow. Disraeli had modernised Conservatism for his time. His ideas of service were reflected in the new public-school ethos and reinforced in the Cambridge history schools, which taught ideals of Christian duty, service to one's fellow men within an organic society where what would now be called active citizenship was an obligation upon every member. The British constitution was the keystone of the nation's greatness, and parliament the indispensable forum for mediating opposing points of view, 'preserving,' as Philip Williamson says in his biography of Baldwin, 'the vital balance between stability and change'. But at Cambridge, Baldwin also learnt that democracy was 'by far the most difficult' form of government, vulnerable to demagoguery and destabilising radicalism, no guarantor of progress. These were themes to which he continually referred in his political career.

To this was added the influence of William Cunningham, the chaplain of his college, Trinity, who became a family friend and officiated at his marriage. The enemy of academic economists, he gave Baldwin the later confidence to draw not on the theories of intellectuals but on his own experience in industry for his understanding of economics, or what Cunningham called 'national husbandry'. In the early years of the 20th century, Cunningham became the leading academic supporter of tariff reform, and theoretician of the empire as a 'Greater Britain', ideas that led later to Empire Free Trade. He was also a friend of Arnold Toynbee, economic historian and founder of the East London settlement Toynbee Hall, where Baldwin had worked during vacations from Cambridge, and he was a stern critic of the materialist aspect of socialism. To Baldwin, who found the term 'capitalist' offensively confrontational, he lent theoretical support for the conviction that the interests of workers and employers were, over time, identical. Cunningham, Williamson argues, 'presented – and probably helped to impress on Baldwin – an economic, moral and Christian Conservatism as the positive and truly national alternative to both Liberalism and socialism.'[8]

There was no question of scouting around for a winnable seat: Baldwin sat for Worcestershire. In 1904 he was selected for what had been, during this period of Tory dominance, a comfortably safe seat at Kidderminster. Unhappily, 1906 was the year of the great Liberal landslide, and Kidderminster, despite Baldwin's assiduous if fastidious attendance at successive local drinking nights for the constituency's 4,500 voters, slid too. The experience of soliciting votes had been so distasteful that Baldwin took off on a 48-hour walk in the Cotswolds to expel it from his system. He was never to enjoy general elections and their attendant requirement to woo the voters. An even greater personal blow followed when he was rejected as candidate by Worcester City, in favour of an Irishman. The hurt Baldwin felt suggests that however noble and public spirited his intentions, he was not without a high degree of personal ambition: *I was turned down*, he told the Classical Association in 1926, *in my own county town, in favour of a stranger and bang went all my hopes.*[9]

I was turned down in my own county town, in favour of a stranger and bang went all my hopes.

BALDWIN

But luck is a politician's greatest asset, and Baldwin, this time in the cruellest way, had it. Early in 1908, suddenly, his father died and, along with his business interests, Baldwin inherited his Bewdley seat. Barely a month later, having stood 'as my father's son', he was returned unopposed. In tribute to the respect won by his father, he was presented to parliament by Austen Chamberlain, scion of the great Birmingham dynasty of Chamberlains. This was something more than a personal gesture. The party remained bitterly divided over tariff reform, a cause that Alfred Baldwin, like most of the West Midland Conservatives, had ardently supported. In industrial seats it was felt that restrictive tariffs were hampering British trade. Imposing tariffs on Britain's own imports would, it was thought, provide a bargaining tool to break down those of other countries. It would also raise revenue that could be used, according to taste, either to reduce the tax burden, or to fund government spending on welfare. Austen Chamberlain had replaced his stricken father Joseph as leader of the reformers, using methods of such dubiety to ensure that his supporters were selected in winnable seats that the independence of local associations was strengthened in an effort to curtail his activities. Baldwin was a welcome recruit to a cause that less than 20 years later nearly destroyed his own political career. Within weeks of his own election, he was speaking at a Manchester by-election for another tariff reformer, William Joynson Hicks, against the free trader Winston Churchill.

Baldwin, now aged 40, a successful businessman, was on his way in politics, but still not clearly resolved on a political career. In fact, he spoke only half a dozen times in as many years. Years later, he described how in his first year as an MP he would go round the Commons armed always with a couple of books under his arm looking for a secluded spot in which to read. 'He felt uncertain and not at home in Parliamentary life, and this was enhanced by a natural shyness.'[10] In his maiden speech he spoke against the introduction of the eight-hour day in the mining industry not because he was opposed to it in principle – his own employees had long enjoyed it – but (illogically) because its cost would bear down too heavily on industries for which coal was a necessary resource. He actively maintained the flourishing business interests that enabled him to buy first a comfortable London house in South Kensington and then to move to even grander surroundings in Eaton Square, where there was more space for entertaining. In an age when Lord Londonderry was accused of dining his way to the Cabinet, this could be seen as a further sign of political ambition, yet, if so, it was curiously unmatched by high profile activity in the House of Commons.

Baldwin steadily gained the reputation of a self-made man with nothing to prove; a flattering and useful attribution of an independent outlook in a prolonged period of opposition.

He made himself liked across the parties, treating Labour members rather as he would workmen at home, choosing their company in the smoking room over members of his own party. He was also active in back-bench party groups like the Unionist (Conservative) Social Reform Committee, which he could afford to sponsor. Yet in the public development of ideas, in the contemporary intellectual debate he was a non-participant. His politics were unusually concerned with the well-being of his constituents, in whose interests, he reported to his mother, he worked steadily. The high politics of party positioning, and of positioning within the party, were not his immediate concern. His anxiety to become an MP suggests that he was aware he had an apprenticeship to serve, one on which he wanted to embark in order to move on to greater things, but he made little visible progress.

Meanwhile business continued to occupy most of his time. He had become a director of the Great Western Railway (his father had been chairman) which introduced him to a different industrial arena where labour relations were far more abrasive than in Baldwin's works at Wilden. The firm's interests in mining and steel production in South Wales were also a practical demonstration of the improbability of realising his ambition of persuading working-class men living in slum housing on poverty wages that their interests were the same as their distant, rich employers and the even more distant and invisible shareholders. Yet in the Commons, Baldwin showed signs of being a reformer. As well as sponsoring the Social Reform committee, he was one of a handful who broke ranks and supported Asquith's old age pensions legislation, although he subsequently protested strongly at higher taxes. It was, he felt, a failure of leadership not to have explained the costs as well as the benefits of higher spending on welfare to the nation. In 1912 when a coal strike forced him to lay off all hands in four different works, a sign went up: *'I do not like to see men who have worked for E.P. & W. Baldwin thrown out of employment through no fault of their own. I therefore hope to make an allowance to every one working for weekly wages ...* '[11] (When the strike was over the workers presented him with an illuminated address in thanks.) From 1914–18, like his father during the Boer War, Baldwin paid the friendly society subscriptions of all his constituents who joined up, ensuring continued sickness and unemployment cover. Most spectacularly, embarrassed by the huge profits made by Baldwin's during the war, he donated a fifth of his fortune anonymously to the Treasury to pay off the war loan and reduce the interest being met by ordinary taxpayers, a gesture that later left him relatively poor. To exhort others to do likewise, he wrote anonymously to the *Times*, signing the letter as 'FST' – he was Financial Secretary to the Treasury – but once again he was to be disappointed by public morality. *How can the nation be made to understand the gravity of the financial situation?* His letter asked rhetorically, *that love of country is better than love of money? This can only be done by example ...* He contributed £120,000 (about £3.5 million at today's prices); his letter prompted another £400,000 of gifts. Goodwill was no alternative to taxation.

In the two elections of 1910 he was returned for Bewdley with an increased majority, having stood as the tariff reform candidate. *It would all be unbearable if it wasn't one's rather obvious duty ...* he wrote to his aunt Edith.[12] It was a period of constitutional uncertainty: the Liberal government challenged the Lords over the budget, while Ireland challenged the constitution over Home Rule. At the same time, industrial relations were becoming increasingly hostile, and the reality of class politics was reflected in the formation and early gains of the Labour Party. There were dockers' and miners' strikes and support grew swiftly for the theory of Direct Action, which envisaged trade unions taking power. Only the outbreak of war in 1914 brought industrial peace.

Reviewing his career 30 years later, Baldwin identified these as the years when, too old to fight, he reconsidered his own future. In 1925 he talked of giving *for the rest of our lives, as a thank-offering to the dead, nothing but the best services we could render to our country.*[13] In 1938, he wrote that in the

There came to me by degrees a changed sense of values, and I began to feel that I might be used for some special work.

BALDWIN

war, he had *found his soul. There came to me by degrees a changed sense of values, and I began to feel that I might be used for some special work.*[14] His nephew, Kipling's son John, died at Loos aged 18. His own son, Oliver, left school early to join up. Oliver was taken aback when his father inquired what kind of memorial he would like if he did not return. In fact he was taken prisoner in the Middle East and like many soldiers, returned unhappy and unsettled.

At the time, far from 'special work', Baldwin considered returning to private life. Lucy had to encourage him to stay in Parliament for the ten years he had always intended. But after the fall of Asquith's coalition in 1916, he joined the Lloyd George coalition government, which rested largely on Conservative support. His standing as a back-bencher and his acknowledged expertise, as a prosperous businessman, was in matters of finance and, after nearly nine years as a back-bench MP (throughout which time, it should be added, his party was either in opposition or at best, coalition), he was invited to serve as parliamentary aide to Bonar Law, the Chancellor of the Exchequer. This entailed deputising for the Financial Secretary, whose role he was soon to take over completely. The work was demanding, requiring financial knowledge as well as the ability to make speeches on complex subjects from the government front bench. He enjoyed it, but in February 1917 it is clear from a letter to his mother that he was still uncertain whether politics were the right course for him. By the 1918 'coupon' election, which renewed the Coalition's hold on power, he appears to have decided. Although denied promotion, he had a new boss as Chancellor, his old ally Austen Chamberlain. Baldwin's rise had been unspectacular, steady rather than eye-catching. Insiders hinted at a future outside the House, appointments abroad, or even the Speakership. He laughed them off. His idea of service did not include governorships of distant provinces. He might also have considered Lucy's appetite for the grandeur and conventions of a foreign post: she had a reputation for gaffes. She once famously announced to a wartime charity function that everyone present should 'be responsible for at least one unmarried mother'.

In March 1921, Bonar Law, already a sick man, retired from the Cabinet and as leader of the Conservative Party, to be succeeded in the Commons by Austen Chamberlain. In the reshuffle that followed Baldwin did not, as he had hoped, get the Chancellorship, but instead was made President of the Board of Trade. Although it was not in the front rank of Cabinet posts, it was a tricky brief in a coalition cabinet split between free traders and tariff reformers. Austen Chamberlain, albeit when trying to prevent the previous incumbent Sir Robert Horne being moved to the Treasury, had called it the most difficult job in government. Baldwin's principle task was to pilot the Safeguarding Bill through the Commons. The Bill was a gesture towards tariff reform which in certain circumstances offered protection to vulnerable industries. The post-war boom was petering out, industrial militancy was approaching its peak, and Baldwin wrote anxiously about the danger of a pool of long-term unemployed. All the old debates about Britain's industrial future and the fate of its workforce, riven with industrial unrest, torn by large-scale unemployment, were reopened. Even when the measure was passed, safeguarding continued to divide the cabinet. Each application to apply duties came before it, to be fought over by the free-trade Liberals (led, on this occasion, by Winston Churchill) and protectionist Conservatives. Over one particular point relating to the importation of fabric gloves from Germany, Baldwin threatened to resign. He got his way. For the first time, he emerged as a champion of traditional Conservatism against the Liberals, and it was noted on the backbenches.

Baldwin in Cabinet was a minor player, remembered more for his silences than his contributions, sometimes almost a figure of fun. But this seemingly underrated figure was about to play a central role in bringing down the sparkling talents of Lloyd George's coalition.

Chapter 2: If you can wait ... (1922–4)

I knew that I had been chosen as God's instrument for the work of the healing of the nation. But you can understand how puzzled I was that He should choose such a specimen of His creatures to work through![1]

In the summer of 1922, Stanley Baldwin was a diligent, respected but unshowy junior cabinet minister, almost unknown outside Westminster, a late middle-aged politician (he was 55 in August) whose political career so far consisted only of a year as President of the Board of Trade and five virtually invisible years as Financial Secretary to the Treasury. A year later he was Prime Minister, and remained so for seven of the next 14 years. No one saw him coming. He would not have predicted it, nor probably desired it, himself. Yet when the coalition fell, he was well positioned for the turn the Conservative Party was about to make. Baldwin wanted the party to rediscover what he considered to be its true principles and values. He was confident that they reflected his own. He had a strong sense of the urgency with which British politics needed to be realigned, a shrewd idea of the mood of the party, and a sense of the proper direction of travel. These are necessary but not sufficient preconditions of success. Baldwin also had luck.

The early 1920s were lived in the shadow of the October 1917 revolution in Russia, when the Bolsheviks had seized power. A fear of Communism, an important factor in the rise to power of Mussolini in 1922 and Hitler in 1933, also dominated British politics. The great question, although the one least openly discussed, was how to halt the rise of Labour. It was a consideration in almost every great political decision after the end of the war and it is the backdrop against which Baldwin's sudden ascent can most readily be understood. Between 1918 and 1922, there were strikes with the overtly political intention of coercing Parliament; trade union Councils of Action were credited with forcing the government to abandon plans to arm the Poles against the Russians; there was a general strike in Glasgow, a police strike in Liverpool and national strikes in the railways and the mines. In by-elections in this period, the Labour party defeated Coalition candidates in 13 seats. Some believed they would emerge from the next election as the largest single party. There was even talk of an overall majority and a Labour government. In 1918, Sidney Webb's mildly socialist constitution held out the prospect of common ownership of the means of production, and was portrayed as a ruthless attack on private property. But the party itself was divided between moderates like Arthur Henderson and J R Clynes, and the much more radical Independent Labour Party whose effective leadership was passing from the cerebral Ramsay MacDonald, out of Parliament from 1918–22, to the fiery Clydesiders like Jimmy Maxton.

Supporters of Lloyd George, hankering after a centre party, believed the more moderate wing of the Labour Party might be detached and introduced into an anti-left coalition. It was felt that of the existing parties and fragments, only the grouping best able to contain Labour could survive. There were Liberals and Conservatives who supported the coalition and Asquithian Liberals and independent Conservatives who did not, and two different die-hard Conservative bodies in the Lords and the Commons.[2] Across these groupings there were shades of opinion reflecting different priorities – the Union and the Constitution, the economy and industry, and in varying degrees, a general lack of enthusiasm for Lloyd George and the compromises of coalition. Under the force of war and democracy, the party system had shattered.

For Austen Chamberlain, Conservative leader in the Commons since the retirement of Bonar Law in 1921, the principle function of the coalition led by Lloyd George was to stand as a barrier between the Labour Party and power. In the course of 1922 however, many of his MPs and much of the party in the country, where the coalition had never been popular, came to believe the reverse. They thought the coalition a liability, and an independent Conservative Party able to argue the Conservative case a more effective weapon. As early as January 1922, the Party Chairman, Sir George Younger, had warned against going into another election as part of the Coalition. Chamberlain seemed deaf to the argument, and was dismissive of the handful of by-election victories won by independent Conservative candidates against the Coalition. Even in October 1922, he was arguing that those who supposed the Conservatives could win alone were 'living in a fool's paradise and ... may easily involve themselves and the country in dangers the outcome of which it is hard to predict'.[3] A series of meetings in the summer intended to convey the disquiet to the leadership succeeded only in driving a wedge deeper between the two parts of the party. At a meeting between party grandees and junior ministers, Lord Birkenhead (the title F E Smith had taken when Lloyd George made him Lord Chancellor in 1919) spoke so rudely to his younger colleagues that many vowed there and then they would never again serve in a government that included him.

Baldwin disliked coalition, and he intensely disliked Lloyd George and his informal *ad hoc* style of government where principle was sacrificed to pragmatism, cabinet was ignored and power resided with an inner core of ministers and quasi-civil servants. Money rather than merit was the motive for appointments: some of the new coalition Conservatives were thought to have paid for their 'coupon' of endorsement from Lloyd George. Baldwin was the 'Conservative friend' quoted in *The Economic Consequences of the Peace* by the economist J M Keynes, for remarking that the 1918 intake looked like men who had done very well out of the war. It was not only Lloyd George's style that was offensive. Baldwin felt he was casually destroying working class confidence in government by abandoning social reform, fudging the question of nationalising the coal mines and bodging compromises to end industrial disputes, all decisions that could only strengthen Labour's appeal. In January he had written *How they are all intriguing ... I want a cleaner atmosphere*.[4] At the height of the scandal over the sale of honours which erupted in the spring, he told that most Conservative of newspapers, the *Morning Post*, what he claimed was an Afghani proverb: *He who lives in the bosom of the Goat* [a reference to Lloyd George] *spends his remaining years plucking out the fleas*. Yet in public he could be heard defending the Coalition. Maurice Cowling[5] found evidence that Lloyd George, aware of the fissiparous nature of his coalition, was wooing him with the prospect of promotion in March, and Baldwin reports breakfasting with him. But in early September he was growing anxious.

> **Baldwin** spent at least a month in Aix-les-Bains, in the foothills of the Alps, every summer from 1921 to 1938. Lucy took the waters while Baldwin walked. *During the fine weather I was out hours a day, and when I had walked myself into a lather, I lay like a lizard in the sun* ...[6] The visits became an event in the spa town's calendar. Latterly, the Baldwins' wedding anniversary, 12 September, became a matter of public celebration.

He retired for his second annual summer retreat to Aix-les-Bains and pondered the future. Towards the end of September, he learned that the Coalition was threatening war to defend Greece against a Turkish resurgence: the British garrison at Chanak on the Dardanelles had been put on alert. For Baldwin, the most significant aspect was talk of a snap election, cynically timed to capitalise on nervousness about the international situation which Austen Chamberlain had sanctioned despite the party's hostility to the continuation of the Coalition. On 29 September, Baldwin was recalled from Aix for an emergency Cabinet session, to be held on Sunday 1 October. He arrived home to find war imminent and Westminster, even though Parliament was not sitting, frothing with rumours of crisis in the Coalition. The war threat passed. The crisis in the coalition did not. Lord Curzon, the Foreign Secretary, watching small groups of ministers huddled in corners, observed: 'The death tick is audible in the rafters.'[7]

Lloyd George had had a bad year, in which his high-handed behaviour over Turkey was only the latest action to offend many Conservatives. Baldwin finally resolved that he could not stay within the Coalition. He was not alone: by mid-October, at least three other ministers were ready to resign. But the big beasts – in particular Chamberlain and also, except when the leadership of a reinvigorated Conservative party was dangled before him, the capricious but charismatic figure of Lord Birkenhead – were signed up to the continuance of the coalition at least until after an election. Anxious to find a way to retain their leaders, the rebels tried to devise a scheme that would satisfy both camps. But a majority of them were determined to campaign independently of the coalition. Chamberlain remained convinced it was a course that would spell disaster.

Baldwin now emerged for the first time as a significant

party figure, a minister in Cabinet who had shown courage in defending Conservative values (over the Safeguarding Bill), who could act as linkman between junior ministers, backbenchers and the leadership. The rebels' objective was to achieve an end to Coalition without splitting the party. The negotiations had at least to appear amicable, and must not become confrontational. They required a respected leader under whom even the grandees would serve. Bonar Law, with whom Baldwin had close connections, was the obvious candidate.

But he was already unwell, and was uncertain about returning to public life in order to fight his old friends. Baldwin met Law on at least two occasions in the run-up to the decisive meeting on the future of the Coalition, which took place at the Carlton Club on 19 October. The meeting had been delayed to hear the result of an impending by-election in Newport, which Labour was expected to win. This was intended to underline the threat the new party posed. Instead the seat was taken by an independent Conservative. Still Chamberlain came to the Carlton Club meeting determined to preserve the coalition.

Andrew Bonar Law, born in 1858, became Conservative Party leader in the Commons in 1911 and was Lloyd George's Chancellor of the Exchequer from 1916–18 and Lord Privy Seal 1918–21 when he resigned through ill health. He was a Glasgow businessman, a teetotal widower, and the first leader of the 'Conservative and Unionist' Party. He died in 1923. (See *Bonar Law* by Andrew Taylor, in this series.)

On 10 October, Baldwin told a meeting of Conservative Coalition Cabinet ministers that he would resign rather than go into an election as a Coalition candidate. When Lucy finally arrived back from France on 12 October, Baldwin told her that he had *done a terrible thing*. It would be the end of his political career, for none of the other Conservative ministers in Cabinet had supported him, although at a second meeting that day, another middle-ranking minister, Arthur Griffith-Boscawen,[8] had said he too would resign. News of Baldwin's stand swiftly spread. By 16 October he had emerged as the senior rebel in a growing revolt to which more recruits were drawn by ill-judged speeches from Chamberlain and Lloyd George defending their handling of the Chanak crisis. Curzon, long frustrated by Lloyd George's tendency to interfere in foreign policy, started to slide towards the rebels. A further random sample of back-bench opinion organised by Baldwin and his parliamentary aide J C C 'David' Davidson produced evidence of strong opposition to the Coalition. But loyalty has always been a powerful weapon in the Conservative Party, especially when backed by offers of honours which, Beaverbrook later wrote, were being sprayed with a hose from Downing Street. Even on the morning of the Carlton Club meeting it was not clear who would win – nor, until the eleventh hour, that their only possible leader, Bonar Law, would feel strong enough to appear. At the end of their final, inconclusive meeting, Baldwin bitterly accused him of *leaving the white men on the beach*.

Chamberlain, who had taken hostility to the Coalition as a personal attack, damaged his position further with a long, unbending speech at the Carlton Club. In reply, Baldwin, announcing himself as the leader of the minority, praised Lloyd George as *a dynamic force*, capable like all such forces of great damage. If the coalition continued, he said, *the old Conservative Party* [will be] *smashed to atoms … I do not know what the majority here or in the country may think about it. I said at the time what I thought was right, and I stick all through to what I believe to be right.*[9] Baldwin's speech was well received. But what decided Lloyd George to resign, before he had even heard the result of the vote, was the arrival at the Carlton

Club of Bonar Law. The Conservatives themselves were less certain. Lucy Baldwin, waiting outside in her car to hear the result, was told the vote was 187 to 87. But she did not know who had won. Only when she reached home again did she discover that the Coalition was defeated. The King sent for Bonar Law and soon afterwards, proposed by Lord Curzon and seconded by Baldwin, Law was elected leader of the newly-entitled 'Conservative and Unionist' Party. Baldwin was offered the Exchequer, but demurred, saying he did not wish to appear to gain from his part in the overthrow of the Coalition. However, when the alternative choice, Reginald McKenna,[10] declined, Baldwin felt able to accept. His career, which barely a week earlier he had thought destroyed, was set on an entirely new trajectory.

For the first time Baldwin's political character emerges. Traits that first appeared in the autumn of 1922 were to become familiar in his years in power: the ruminating over the decision, the long, contemplative walks, the tendency to wait and watch before acting, the sensitivity to the mood of the party – and then his ability, with his back to the wall, to pull off an exceptional speech, like the one he made in the Carlton Club and as he was to do to great effect at critical moments in the future. Even the nature of the crisis – which he saw as a constitutional matter – can be seen as typical of the kind that most powerfully affected his sense of political leadership.

It is never easy to judge the importance of a single individual in a party crisis, where official papers are scarce and memoirs are heavily laced with hindsight. Middlemas and Barnes thought his speech of resignation to the Conservative cabinet ministers on 10 October was 'probably the most politically courageous act' of his life. At that point, although he was already aware of the mood in the party, it was unclear how it would be resolved. The coalition had, after all, been unpopular with Conservatives from the moment of the 1918 election. Earlier eruptions of discontent had been suppressed. This revolt too might have come to nothing. It seems, therefore, that Baldwin genuinely believed, as he told Lucy, he was hazarding his political future. But a good resignation is a powerful political weapon. However, Sir George Younger, the chairman, thought 'the party was stampeding'.[11] Baldwin must also have known that if the Coalition did collapse, he would be at the forefront of Conservative politics. In the more cynical eyes of Maurice Cowling, 'Baldwin's significance arose from the fact that he played a leading part in amalgamating the various sentiments of Conservative resistance of which his own was a typical and apparently instinctive example.'[12]

Nor should Lucy Baldwin's role in her husband's political life be overlooked, for she was an intense if vicarious participant at least in those party aspects where she was able to play a role. Despite their contrasting personalities, Lucy practical and active, Stanley contemplative and bookish, they were a good match. Bound together by their religious faith (despite differing styles of observance, for Lucy was Low Church and Stanley High) they prayed together every morning, she once confided to an ambassador's wife, seeking God's guidance for the day ahead. They grew to look alike: he rumpled and pipe-smoking, she, a little dowdy, with a taste for unusual hats. Yet there was a strong ambition for her husband that more than once kept him in politics where without her encouragement he might have withdrawn. From a political family but excluded from direct involvement in political life herself, she cared probably more passionately than he about Conservative party politics, actually defacing photographs of Lloyd George that she had earlier collected in an album. To Baldwin's reserve she applied energetic resolve. A lifelong diarist, in the account of the crisis she wrote a month or so after it was resolved, she wrote boldly, 'THE RECOLLECTIONS OF A CABINET BREAKER'S WIFE ON THE GOVERNMENT CRISIS, OCTOBER 1922'.

Law's cabinet was, with the exception of Curzon who remained Foreign Secretary, bereft of the big names that had dominated politics for the previous five years. It was dubbed the 'second eleven'. Nonetheless, at the election that Bonar Law immediately called, fighting on a platform of safety and tranquillity, the coalition-breakers were triumphantly vindicated. Their total of 344 seats was exaggerated by the fragmentation of the opposition, with two Liberal parties as well as Labour fighting (the Tory share of the vote was less than 40 per cent). But it was claimed as a mandate for traditional Conservatism. There was one exception. In the course of the campaign, Bonar Law had expressly ruled out tariff reform without a further appeal to the people. Some believed the pledge had been an important factor in delivering the traditional free trade areas like Lancashire into Conservative hands. Whether or not it was true, the idea achieved a status that within a year was to be a heavy burden.

Baldwin's experience as a businessman and then in politics as Financial Secretary and President of the Board of Trade gave him at least a familiarity with the work of the Treasury. But the problems that he faced were as much political as financial. The deficit of £65 million, (around £2 billion in 2006 prices) was uncomfortably large. Baldwin immediately sent warning notes to all the spending ministers. But the severe dislocation of international trade, caused by the burden of war debt and reparations, was the greatest drain on the British economy. The number of jobless in January 1923 was more than 1.5 million, of whom nearly a third were war veterans. Baldwin's immediate tasks, with preparations for a spring budget already underway, were to cut back spending and try to hack a path through the thickets of German insolvency, the French appetite for revenge (in January 1923, they marched into the Ruhr to expropriate coal in lieu of the reparations Germany could not afford to pay), and American isolationism that curtailed any action by the US administration to renegotiate the war loans.

Most pressing of these was the war loans question, for a meeting in America had already been delayed by the election. Straight after Christmas, Baldwin set sail for the United States, accompanied by his wife, one of his daughters and the Governor of the Bank of England, Montagu Norman. Britain needed to renegotiate the outstanding $3 billion loan made by America during the war for goods purchased in the US for the Allied war effort with British credit. The current terms were so onerous that Britain had had to suspend interest payments almost as soon as they had been negotiated, and they had been resumed only in October 1922. There was an aggrieved feeling at home that Britain was being unjustly made to foot the bill for defeating Germany, despite the failure of the Allies to repay Britain, caused by Germany's inability to pay reparations. But expounding British difficulties made no difference to Germany's capacity to meet the Versailles obligations and further soured public opinion in the US where Britain's grievances merely appeared rude and ungrateful. *Of course we shall pay. But we think you are cads to ask us*, was Baldwin's précis of the position. Law, who thought the only just solution was the cancellation of all debts, had given Baldwin some leeway to reach an agreement on the twin issues of the rate of interest and the length of repayment. Baldwin could not get a deal within the bounds set by Bonar Law, but after a week of negotiation, he believed he had the best deal on offer (and a good deal better than the existing terms),

American Debt Settlement

The novel feature of post-war unemployment was that it continued at a permanently high level. There was little hint of this as the immediate post-war boom, based on a universal desire to replenish stocks, got underway in 1919–1920. The boom was helped by the Government's decision not to restore the gold standard, suspended during the war. This would have involved violent deflation, and to start the peace with a depression seemed an appalling prospect. However, the Government took fright at the rapid inflation which on the Continent foreshadowed the collapse of most Central European currencies. The Bank Rate was put up to 6 per cent in November 1919, and to 7 per cent the following April. In 1921 unemployment in Britain rose to 19 per cent. Recovery when it came was slow and limited. The 1913 level of production was not regained until 1927. Unemployment from 1922 to 1929 remained about 10 per cent. Mass unemployment was initially explained by the dislocation of the international trading monetary systems caused by the First World War. Hence the aim of the British government was to restore as swiftly as possible the pre-war trading and monetary structure. This involved currency stabilization (via a return to the gold standard) and the reduction of tariffs put up during and immediately after the war.

However, as the decade wore on it became increasingly apparent that Britain's leading export industries were being hit, not only post-war dislocations, but also by long-term changes in demand which the war doubtless accelerated. 'Back to 1914' would not solve the problems facing the coal, textile, and heavy engineering industries, where the bulk of the unemployed were concentrated. Moreover, the return to the gold standard in 1925 hindered the development of new industries and the rationalization of old ones by creating monetary stringency at a time when plentiful credit was needed for adaptation to the new conditions ... the climate of opinion the 1920s favoured a swift return to laissez-faire, and this dictated the course of British economic policy. [Robert Skidelsky, *Politicians and the Slump* (Macmillan, London: 1967) Chapter 1] especially since it was understood that acceptance would further his long-term objective of securing US help to restore financial stability in Europe. Moreover, he understood the terms were likely to worsen as US elections loomed. Finally, a failure to settle would look as if England were defaulting, with severe consequences for her creditworthiness. Bonar Law – backed by Keynes – thought the terms unacceptable, and recalled Baldwin to London. On arrival, he caused a scandal by casually revealing the deal he had negotiated and describing it as the best that he could get, before adding, possibly off the record, that the Americans had a problem with mid-Western congressmen and their constituents who had no understanding of international finance. This view was rapidly translated back in the States as an attack on hicks from the sticks that caused great public offence. Although there is no evidence either way, it is possible that Baldwin wanted British public opinion to understand the difficulties the Americans faced.

Baldwin, notorious for avoiding fights if at all possible, failed to defend the terms at a private meeting with Bonar Law. But at a full Cabinet meeting on 30 January, they argued openly. Law, Chancellor himself at the time the original terms had been negotiated, declared Baldwin's terms would impose an unjust burden on generations of British taxpayers (the debt was to be repaid over 63 years), one that would prevent tax cuts or any reduction in the cost of living. Warning that the terms were so adverse his name would be cursed down the years, he threatened to resign. Only when it became apparent that City as well as political opinion was in favour of acceptance did he agree to stay. Baldwin, who from his earliest promotion to his current role as Chancellor owed much to Bonar Law, was nevertheless prepared to lead the Cabinet against him. Beaverbrook, one of Bonar Law's closest friends, claimed later the episode so distressed Bonar Law that it shortened his life.

There were few other recorded instances of Baldwin adopting such an uncompromising stance.

In the Commons the following month, he caused a great public stir with a speech defending the government's position in Europe and the relationship between its policy there and the prospects for employment at home. Having set out the need to achieve stability in order to revitalise trade, which in turn would restore British industry, he turned the attack to the Left, and to Communism. Scoffing at foreign, pentasyllabic words like 'proletariat', he declared: *The English language is the richest in the world in monosyllables. Four words, of one syllable each, are words which contain salvation for this country and for the whole world, and they are 'faith', 'hope', 'love' and 'work'. No Government in this country today which has not faith in the people, hope in the future, love for its fellow men, and which will not work, and work and work, will ever bring this country though into better days and better times, or will ever bring Europe through, or the world through.*

Four words, of one syllable each, are words which contain salvation for this country and for the whole world, and they are 'faith', 'hope', 'love' and 'work'.

BALDWIN

It was the first sign that Baldwin could convey sentiments not normally heard from politicians, in language that was at once simple and subtle, and spoke directly to ordinary people. Honesty, decency and plain speaking, often with a dose of sentiment. It was to be a winning combination.

Bonar Law was ill. The two years of health that his doctor had given him when he resumed the leadership seemed already to have been over-optimistic. In the Commons, Baldwin deputised for him as well as preparing his first and, it turned out, his only budget which he delivered on 16 April. Within a month, barely two years after first entering the Cabinet, he would be Prime Minister.

Part Two

THE LEADERSHIP

Chapter 3: If you can dream ... (1923–4)

I have never had any ambitious plans and I do not know how
it has come about that I am the Prime Minister of England.
To me it is very strange.[1]

On 11 May 1923, little more than six months after assuming
office, Bonar Law was diagnosed with throat cancer. In Paris
at the time, the news of his resignation preceded his return to
London on 20 May. He was entitled to make a recommendation on the succession to the King, George V, but he let it be
known that he would prefer not to be consulted. The choice
was not an easy one. The party's acknowledged star, Austen
Chamberlain, remained unreconciled to the breaking of the
Coalition. Lord Curzon, Marquess Curzon of Kedleston,
Foreign Secretary, former Viceroy of India, brilliant, vain,
difficult,[2] and above all, a member of the House of Lords
where Labour was unrepresented, had already irritated Bonar
Law by writing to set out his claims.

And there was Baldwin, untested, almost unknown outside
Westminster, yet who in the past six months seemed hardly
to have made a misjudgement, slipping with ease into the
role of Prime Minister in Bonar Law's absence.

In his house in Onslow Gardens, the dying Bonar Law wrote
by hand to the King to tender his resignation. Meanwhile his
private secretary, Baldwin's ally and now a backbench MP,

J C C Davidson,[3] was dictating a second document setting out, he later insisted, a backbencher's (and not Bonar Law's) views of the succession. Without making a recommendation, this unsigned document strongly favoured Baldwin. It was taken, without further explanation, together with the resignation letter, to the King, thus prompting years of historical wrangling about the propriety and independence of the King's ultimate decision. For two days, all political society held its breath. Lord Salisbury rushed up from the country in the guard's van of the milk train to offer advice. Lord Curzon, at his house in Montacute in Somerset where he had elected not to install a telephone, awaited the telegraphic summons and planned his first Cabinet. Early on the morning of 22 May, he set off by train for London. That afternoon, the King sent for Baldwin and invited him to form a government. 'Mr Stanley Baldwin ... is much liked by all shades of political opinion in the House of Commons, and has the complete confidence of the City and the commercial world generally. He in fact typifies the spirit of the government which the people of this country elected last autumn ... ie honesty, simplicity, and balance.' Davidson's encomium of the man who had already become a surrogate father to himself and his wife, Baldwin's walking companion, Mimi, was not unbiased, but nor was

Curzon never quite shook off a ditty from his Oxford days: 'My name is George Nathaniel Curzon/I am a most superior person./ My cheeks are pink, my hair is sleek,/I dine at Blenheim once a week.' Bonar Law was much amused, a few months earlier, when Curzon had arrived at a meeting in Paris in a great temper after the authorities in Clermont-Ferrand had refused to stop the trams in order to allow him a properly restful night. Baldwin once declared Curzon had *given me the kind of greeting a corpse gives an undertaker.*

it undeserved. G M Young, whose biography of Baldwin, despite being officially commissioned was generally unfavourable, depicted him as 'a fond projection of everything that the common Englishman still believed himself to be. Within a few months the lonely Prime Minister was what no man in that place had ever been before, a household figure, almost a family friend'.[4]

The new Prime Minister, not quite 55, was stocky and rather pale with the reddish hair that betrayed the Celtic origins of his mother. G M Young described 'a humorous mouth that could close with a snap, blue eyes under shaggy brows ... his voice: crisp, musical, far carrying: with a harsh note in reserve if a topic was to be ended, an intruder silenced, or a suggestion dismissed'.[5] Austen Chamberlain once warned him against levity, Bonar Law against excessive modesty. He had been delighted to join the Travellers' Club, where for the rest of his political career he often lunched alone and undisturbed. Even as Prime Minister, he continued his habit of spending hours on the government front bench in the Commons, sometimes apparently just browsing in *Dodd's Parliamentary Companion*. Once a colleague looked to see what was occupying him. Baldwin looked up: *I think we should stand a very good chance of winning Caernarvon Boroughs*, he said.[6]

He soon gained a reputation for indolence that he never shed (his 1987 biographer Roy Jenkins, himself an advocate of the short working day during his time as Home Secretary and then Chancellor in the 1960s, gives a succinct summary of Baldwin's style: 'His desk application was poor, but his recreations were semi-political'[7]), but Baldwin had a good brain and a reputation among his officials for being a swift assessor of his papers. Decisions came harder. He read widely, walked and prayed, he talked haphazardly to his small group of intimate friends, enjoyed music and loved his family. This final attribute included even his troubled elder son Oliver, who was making his father miserable by taking up Labour politics, emerging in the pages of the *Evening Standard* during the 1923 election as a Marxist.

Reticence together with an appetite for power are a curious combination to find at the top of politics. Only months earlier, Baldwin had told Davidson he would prefer a one-way ticket to Siberia to the leadership of the party, but Maurice Cowling's feline instincts suggest he was party to a conspiracy to achieve it. It fits ill with his public character, unless he felt some responsibility for the swirling connections at the heart of party politics, where Chamberlain, Birkenhead, Sir Robert Horne and a handful of other senior figures appeared to be preparing to capture the Conservatives for an unspecified but different kind of politics, and grandees like Lords Salisbury and Derby considered branching off in yet another direction. Certainly, on the day of his appointment, he appealed to journalists not for their congratulations but their prayers. A powerful sense of personal responsibility and duty seems to have driven him to overcome the nervousness and tension, the outward signs of which were often observed. He had curious facial tics, a habit of sniffing papers, and often collapsed after periods of intense strain. Baldwin's duty, as he saw it, was to make the greatest contribution he could to the kind of politics he believed England deserved.

'His desk application was poor, but his recreations were semi-political.'

ROY JENKINS ON BALDWIN

I am not a bit excited and don't realise it in the least,[8] he wrote to his mother on the night of his appointment. A conversation a little later with a political opponent, the Asquithian Liberal MP Sir Donald Maclean, left the latter convinced that Baldwin 'had been led to his present position by single-minded devotion to honour and to duty'.[9] Much later, approaching the end of his 14 years at the forefront of British politics, he wrote to his daughter Monica on the theme that underlay much of what he sought to do as Prime Minister, *You see my job is to try and educate a new democracy in a new world and to try and make them realise their responsibilities in their possession of power, and to keep the eternal verities before them.*[10]

Baldwin set out deliberately to distance himself in every respect from Lloyd George. He was consciously anti-intellectual, preferring character to brains, and decency over party. J M Keynes who had originally been attracted to Baldwin's 'decency' soon lost patience. 'There was an attraction at first that Mr Baldwin should not be clever. But when he forever sentimentalises about his own stupidity, the charm is broken.'[11] Baldwin distrusted coalition not because he believed one party had a monopoly on truth but because within it, people were not free to act according to principle. He considered Lloyd George dishonest. Politics in its widest and perhaps most ambitious sense – the shaping of the nation's political culture – led him beyond the boundaries of his party to the people at large.

He was concerned that Labour appeared the party of modernisation. If it was the human losses in war that gave Baldwin political focus, it was its political, social and economic dislocation afterwards that as prime minister became his governing preoccupations. He knew that the clock could not be turned back. He thought it essential that it should not be allowed to spin forward faster than the newly enfranchised masses could be educated into understanding the choices that they had to make. Baldwin wanted to create space for the nation to catch its breath and look around, a period of stability where nerves could be soothed and ambitions, currently attracted to extremes, more modestly directed.

I want to see, Baldwin said in his first major address as Prime Minister, *a better feeling between all classes of our people. If there are those who want to fight the class war we will take up the challenge, and we will beat them by the hardness of our heads and the largeness of our hearts ... I want to be a healer.*[12]

It was not only the class war that concerned him, however. He detected what he termed cultural fragility. It was not the outward signs – the women in short skirts and short hair, who worked for a living and went out on their own. Nor was it increasing prosperity where car ownership rose rapidly, and the use of telephones, and a new mass media that sped up the rate of communication at a rate bewildering to those who grew up in the mid-Victorian era. Electric light and electric fires, the wireless and refrigerators – the revolution was consumerist and, for millions, liberating in the most basic of ways. At least in the prosperous south, a utopia of well-being suddenly seemed almost within reach. Later Baldwin spoke in apocalyptic terms of the menace of a war that would destroy civilisation. In the 1920s, the apocalypse he feared would be wrought by spiritual collapse, the rise of materialism, the destruction of moral standards. He identified another revolutionary era like that of the late 18th century, he wrote of *walking on a thin*

In 1918 the expanded franchise had doubled the electorate.[13] Within three years, hundreds of thousands of these new voters were out of work. At its peak in 1921, TUC conference delegates represented six million members. Trade union membership was at a height not equalled again until the 1960s. The Communist Party of Great Britain was formed in 1920. In 1921 it had seemed the transport workers, the dockers and the railwaymen might strike in sympathy with the miners, producing what could be a revolutionary climate. The security service MI5 regularly reported seditious attempts to subvert soldiers and sailors.

crust beneath which chaos and anarchy seethed. He feared the destructive nature of class politics, believed in a Conservative working class wrongly driven into the arms of Labour by ill-judged actions such as the repeal of trade union protection and inadequate attention to social questions.

Although Baldwin wrote privately *I dread the mass mind*, it was not his style to rail publicly against change and modernisation. Instead in person and in speech he stood for the traditional (often conflated with the rural and the agricultural, to which he believed all men retained an atavistic link). He praised the quality of endurance and the value of the enduring. Seeking to address the widest possible audience, he spoke and wrote beyond conventional political forums, devoting days of effort to a Rectoral address at Edinburgh, or to the introduction for a new cricket anthology. His 'healing mission' in government would seek both to remove the causes of discontent and also to protect and strengthen the institutions that underpinned society.

His more immediate task was unity in his party, starting with his disappointed rival. Lord Curzon, after a day sitting immobile with shock at Baldwin's preferment ('He's nothing! Nothing! Nothing!' he was said to have exclaimed), recovered himself and agreed to continue as Foreign Secretary. Lord Curzon's nobility deprived Baldwin of a carrot to dangle before Austen Chamberlain, for whom there was now no job likely to lure him back into the political mainstream. Baldwin was determined not to allow those who had clung to the coalition back as a group, displacing his own loyalists, effectively naming their price. But for a man so effective in public, Baldwin found personal relationships difficult and he often created problems through his own clumsiness. Austen Chamberlain was easy to offend, but he was already upset that Baldwin behind his back had offered the Treasury to another

Chamberlainite, Sir Robert Horne. Horne, who had no time for Baldwin, refused. Chamberlain complained later that 'I had felt at the time I had been subjected to great and public indignity.'[14] In the end, Baldwin's attempts at restoring unity netted only one middle-ranking coalitionist, Sir Lamming Worthington-Evans. On one level it was a failure, for it meant front rank Conservative politicians might yet stray into Lloyd George's orbit. But for a man so little known outside, and so scornfully dismissed by the Chamberlainites within, it was important to establish that he alone would make his Cabinet.

Meanwhile, Baldwin decided to act as his own Chancellor in the hope that within a matter of months, his second choice, Reginald McKenna, would have recovered from the illness that was keeping him out of public life. With the Budget out of the way, the main preoccupation of the Treasury was the detailed negotiations for settlement of the American war loan. And that tied in closely with what Baldwin considered the most pressing problem facing his new government, bringing stability to Europe, the first step in restoring trade and thus employment in Britain.

France's occupation of the Ruhr continued; relations with Britain remained bad. As the value of the mark tumbled, Germany became worryingly unstable. Baldwin resolved to try to rescue the old Entente, to charm France into a frame of mind where a settlement of the reparations question could be approached, to take advantage of the new American willingness, in the shape of General Dawes, to contribute to a solution to Germany's inability to meet reparations. On his way back from Aix in early October, he stopped in Paris for a face-to-face encounter with the French Prime Minister, Raymond Poincaré. At the end of the meeting, Baldwin believed he had agreement that if Germany ended passive resistance in the Ruhr, France would negotiate. Germany fulfilled its side of the bargain. France reneged. The honeymoon Baldwin had been enjoying with the British press ended in brutal criticism of his diplomacy (encouraged by Birkenhead). Baldwin never again ventured into direct contact with foreign leaders. (Although *Ribbentrop once lunched*, he told G M Young, *and recited* Mein Kampf.[15]).

Baldwin came to have a reputation for extreme hesitancy in making decisions. But in his first months as Prime Minister, his style seemed quite the reverse. 'He takes a leap in the dark,' was another of Birkenhead's complaints before they had been reconciled, 'looks around and takes another.'[16] In the autumn of 1923, Baldwin took a leap the consequences of which were so nearly disastrous that he never took another to match it.

Protection, or tariff reform, after the divisions within the party of the 1900s, had become a subject on which the party agreed to disagree, with the weight of opinion for it but some important voices (notably Lancashire's Lord Derby) against it. But it was the only distinctive answer the Conservatives had to Britain's industrial weakness. In the uncertain political mood left by the years of coalition, Bonar Law had pledged not to introduce it rather than risk what had previously proved an electorally-unpopular policy. But, perhaps frustrated by the slow haul of bringing stability to Europe and the difficulty of achieving his other objective, the restoration of trade with Russia, Baldwin retreated to Aix in 1923 to consider whether its time had finally come. A fortnight's hard walking left him convinced it was the right way forward. The problem was Bonar Law's pledge. *I am not a man to play with a pledge*, he reminded his party conference in October. By then

I am not a man to play with a pledge.

BALDWIN

he had almost certainly decided he had no option but to stake everything on an election.

Like his determination to resign from Lloyd George's Coalition, the decision to advocate protection was not the bombshell it now appears. But nor was it a policy at the forefront of the public mind. Some Conservatives, like Leo Amery who was First Lord of the Admiralty, had never abandoned advocacy of the cause. Baldwin had always been sympathetic. During his business career, E P & W Baldwin Ltd had lost thousands of pounds worth of orders when America imposed high tariffs on iron and steel. Traditionally, tariffs were thought to help industry, government and workers. Protected, industry would win a chance to modernise and rationalise; jobs would be secured; and government had a weapon, a bargaining counter, to negotiate away the tariff barriers increasingly erected by other industrialised countries. To some politicians, protection had the additional merit of raising revenue that could be used to ease the tax burden handicapping industrial development. Joseph Chamberlain, Austen's father, had developed the thesis that it could protect employment too, and in 1923 the prognosis for unemployment, which had lessened marginally during 1922, was bleak. Even the long-awaited resumption of normal trading conditions in Europe, Cabinet was told, would not resolve the problem.

Baldwin wanted to reconstruct his Cabinet. He wanted to bring back the excluded talent. He wanted to prevent Lloyd George, rumoured to be planning a centre party on a protectionist ticket, manoeuvring into a position from which he might once again challenge for power. From within, Curzon lectured him on his weakness over foreign policy, from without, Lord Birkenhead bent the willing ear of Lord Rothermere and of his leading paper, the *Daily Mail*, with attacks on an alleged bias against the French. In private, he encouraged Austen Chamberlain to believe that Rothermere was 'pinning his fortunes on you'. In early October, an Imperial Conference heard calls for imperial preference from the prime ministers of Canada, Australia and South Africa. Tariff Reform had the appeal of the mythical silver bullet, the single policy that could be sold to the country as a panacea for unemployment while rallying all true Conservatives to a cause that distinguished it from Liberals and Labour. Lloyd George would be left in the cold, the Asquithians gently but firmly isolated in the Free Trade corner ('He wanted Asquith on a pedestal, and Lloyd George in an isolation hospital,' Roy Jenkins thought.[17]), Labour would be soundly defeated.

Throughout the autumn there was an elaborate courtship of the coalitionists, facilitated by Austen's half-brother, Neville Chamberlain, who had become – Baldwin having given up waiting for McKenna – Chancellor of the Exchequer. On 25 October, Baldwin told the Party Conference that unemployment was the crucial problem. *If I can fight it, I am willing to fight it. I cannot fight it without weapons. I have for myself come to the conclusion ... if we go on pottering along as we are we shall have grave unemployment with us to the end of time, and I have come to the conclusion myself that the only way of fighting this subject is by protecting the home market.*[18] By the first week in November, he was moving towards an early election. By 12 November, he was appealing to George V for a dissolution. It was the most headstrong and decisive action he took in office.

The decision was taken against the advice of a minority of Cabinet, who wanted a longer campaign to win public understanding and to develop the policy. Lord Curzon was merely the most truculent in his complaints of the 'recklessness' with which both government and country against their will 'have been plunged into a General Election by the arbitrary fiat of one weak and ignorant man'.[19] Even the King expressed his unhappiness at dissolving Parliament barely a year after its election. Curzon was not alone in protesting that it looked like 'trickery'. In fact, it was more widely seen (even by Lloyd George who wrote an extraordinary letter: 'To have become Prime Minister and be retiring to risk it all in favour of a great policy is fine ...') as proof of Baldwin's sincerity and honesty, if not his judgement.

Polling day was 6 December 1923.[20] Baldwin's comfortable majority was turned into a deficit of nearly a hundred. Eighty-seven Conservatives (including Baldwin's loyal aide Davidson) lost their seats. Most alarming of all, given Liberal acquiescence, Labour could form a government. Baldwin appeared to have achieved the very result his critics had predicted, an outcome that Churchill depicted as 'a serious national misfortune such as has usually befallen great States only on the morrow of defeat in war'. In fact the Conservatives had won almost exactly the same share of the vote as a year earlier and because of the first-past-the-post electoral system, still won a disproportionate number of seats, but a reunited Liberal Party and a steadily-growing Labour Party had eaten into their lead.

For a day or two it seemed Baldwin's meteoric rise had ended in disaster. He considered resignation. The Chamberlainites tried to bounce him into it, clearing the way for a return to coalition. Instead, supported by Asquith (who was resisting hysterical appeals to block Labour and save the nation) he resolved to meet Parliament in anticipation of a defeat on the King's Speech leaving Labour to form a government, 'too weak to do much harm but not too weak to get discredited,'[21] as Neville Chamberlain predicted. Baldwin resisted calls for his resignation; but had to make concessions. He brought back all the Chamberlainites including the reviled Birkenhead, in one group, installing them in his 'shadow' cabinet, a forum which had been redundant during the Coalition years. The policy of tariff reform was once more abandoned. From the ashes of defeat, Baldwin emerged with a united party and, despite Chamberlain's frequent references to his group's ability to make things impossible for him, a grip on the leadership.

The scenario of Labour in government that had been painted by the alarmists – that it would bring forward a capital levy, be defeated in Parliament and go to the country to seek a mandate to destroy capitalism – never, of course, came to pass. Baldwin and Ramsay MacDonald had maintained cordial relations in the past and they continued when MacDonald became prime minister. Even the radical ILP MPs had a high regard for Baldwin as an individual that was only strengthened by his refusal to seek to deny them office in 1924. MacDonald's mission, as Baldwin had anticipated, was to prove that his party was fit to govern. MacDonald and his Chancellor, the ascetic Philip Snowden, took a rigidly orthodox view of economics and to the bewilderment of the left were enthusiastic participants in the rigmarole of court presentations and audiences with the King. To the irritation of his more carnivorous colleagues, Baldwin – who had appreciated Asquith's kindness to him in his own early days as Prime Minister[22] – was careful to attack only the ideas, not the men.

Labour's position was almost impossible, in power at the whim of the Liberals, unable to enact radical policies and lacking almost all government experience. Only the radical, John Wheatley, as Housing Minister and MacDonald, acting as his own Foreign Secretary, had some success. In its essentials, MacDonald's interpretation of the European situation differed little from Baldwin's, but he scored the notable victory of resolving the crisis in the Ruhr. He also negotiated treaties with Soviet Russia intended to lead to the restoration of diplomatic relations, a move profoundly unpopular in the country and among both Liberals and Conservatives. By September, it seemed it was the issue on which the government would fall. But through that autumn a scandal emerged that could hardly have done more damage to Labour, nor played to greater advantage to the anti-Socialist forces.

The details of the Campbell affair belong elsewhere. The politics of the matter were that MacDonald appeared to have interfered with the course of justice by preventing the prosecution of a Communist, J R Campbell, for the publication of a seditious entreaty to the armed forces not to fire on their working-class brothers and sisters in the event of a strike or civil unrest. MacDonald, confused, tired and guilty, denied it. Baldwin did not want it to be the issue on which they went to the country. On 7 October, he told the King's private secretary, Lord Stamfordham, that he wanted to turn the government out on the Russian issue, not Campbell. *He considers the P.M. instead of smashing his extremists has allowed them to smash him. He likes and trusts the P.M. [. . .] & always gathered that the P.M. would adopt a quiet yet determined opposition to Communism, believing that in 5 years or so it would die out: but apparently he has not carried out this policy.*[23] In the light of the conduct of the election campaign, this is a significant document. For only if Baldwin genuinely believed that Labour was in thrall to the Communists is it possible to justify his conduct of the final days of the election campaign that began in the second week of October.

Baldwin would lament later that he was a bad Leader of the Opposition. But in the course of the first part of 1924 he had made a series of ten major speeches describing – as the manifesto was later called – the *Aims and Principles* of his Conservative Party that set the framework for the next 13 years. This was modernisation with bite, a programme that introduced to mainstream Conservatism a new concern for the interests of the masses – housing and factory legislation, insurance against sickness and old age – and a commitment to the role of the state in addressing them. He instructed his party to take down the barriers to the broadest choice of candidates by ending the demand that they must underwrite the expenses of their Conservative associations. He warned the electorate that freedom without duty was licence: they had the freedom to vote, and their duty was to vote, and to vote responsibly. He attacked Labour for risking the empire by disarmament, and he established self-government as the objective for India. Above

To me England is the country and the country is England.

BALDWIN

all, he emphasised that national unity was essential, class hatred, fatal. The series of speeches ended with his celebrated address to the Royal Society of St George on 'England and the English Character', the speech which made him famous not as a political leader, but as an Englishman. *To me England is the country and the country is England ... the sounds of England, the tinkle of the hammer on the anvil in the country smithy, the corncrake on a dewy morning, the sound of a scythe against a whetstone, and the sight of a plough team coming over the brow of a hill, the sight that has been seen in England since England was a land ...* [24]

Baldwin presented himself, modestly, as the embodiment of the virtues that he preached. First and foremost, he was an Englishman, tied to a small piece of the land (to the ten miles, he once said, that could be travelled by a horse and carriage); he had devoted his life to service. *I am just one of yourselves, who has been called to special work for the country at this time. I never sought office ... .* [25] Through his conduct in opposing coalition, risking all on an election rather than breaking a pledge, and finally allowing, in a spirit of fair play, Labour to attempt to govern, he had established himself as straight and honest.

How powerful, then, his position when during the 1924 campaign he taunted Labour for being in thrall to the Russians, calling for the party to *rid itself of the extremist forces which appear to control it*. Gregory Zinoviev, chairman of the Communist International, was identified as the principle conduit of the subversion of Britain. In vain did the Labour conference, rattled by the attacks, declare membership of the Communist Party incompatible with membership of Labour. In the final days of the campaign, Baldwin joined a sustained assault led by Conservative Central Office. *It makes my blood boil to read of the way in which Mr Zinoviev is speaking of the Prime Minister today. Though one time there went up a cry, 'Hands off Russia', I think it's time somebody said to Monsieur Zinoviev, 'Hands off England'.*[26] Four days before polling day, the *Daily Mail* published what it claimed was a letter from Zinoviev to the Communist Party of Great Britain that had been intercepted, praising the Russian treaties MacDonald had negotiated for the help they offered the revolution and urging mutiny in the armed forces. Conservatives have always insisted that at the time, they believed the letter genuine. However, in 1927 large sums of money changed hands in payment to the agent who provided it. Research in the 1970s revealed that the letter was almost certainly the work of Poles determined to prevent the restoration of trade and diplomatic relations with Russia.

On 29 October, Baldwin was returned to power with 48 per cent of the vote and a majority of more than 200 over all other parties in the Commons.[27] The Liberal Party was destroyed, reduced to a rump of just 40 MPs to the Conservatives' 419. Labour lost 50 seats. Baldwin was back in Downing Street at the head of a united party. He had won his own mandate. He was no longer the accidental prime minister.

Chapter 4: Triumph (1924–6)

Ten months after the humiliation of December 1923, Baldwin's party had not just recovered but won 2.5 million more votes. Baldwin was in command even of the most awkward talents in his party. The most glittering star, Winston Churchill, who had left the Conservatives to defend free trade with the Liberals in 1906, had returned to the fold. Baldwin had begun the process of modernisation of the party's internal structure and had stamped its policies with his own cast of mind. At the same time he was established in the country as a man of honour, a protector of liberty and guarantor of the English way of life against the vivid threat of subversion. It was a formidable achievement for a man until recently regarded by his critics as a blank in the political firmament.

'To him who lost and fell – who rose and won,

Because his aim was other than men's praise,

This for an omen that in all things done Strength shall be born of unselfseeking days.'

RUDYARD KIPLING.[1]

His Cabinet-making reflected his authority. An ailing Lord Curzon reluctantly took the role of Lord Privy Seal, thus making the Foreign Office available for Austen Chamberlain (until William Hague and his successors the only Conservative Party leader never to be prime minister). Birkenhead, whose drinking and general moral conduct Baldwin had thought made him unfit for high office, was restored to become Secretary of State for India. Another leading Chamberlainite, Sir William Joynson-Hicks, went to the Home Office. But the appointment that shocked the party was the elevation of Churchill to be Chancellor of the Exchequer. Churchill, offered the chance to redeem his father's reputation in the post, was in return even prepared to accept that some industries would require protection. In political terms, it was an inspired appointment, on which Baldwin plunged without consultation between Churchill's arrival at Number Ten and Neville Chamberlain's departure ten minutes earlier saying he did not want the Treasury and preferred to go to Health (he already had in mind a process of reform advancing the welfare state that required 25 bills). Churchill's 'hundred horsepower mind'[2] that so alarmed Baldwin was kept fully occupied and his loyalty was assured.

The weakness of the appointment was Churchill's ignorance of economics. It made it hard to escape the confines of Treasury orthodoxy. Almost at once, he had to make the single biggest economic decision of the inter-war years, whether sterling should return to the gold standard, and at what rate. The 'if' was almost beyond dispute: it had been an objective of economic policy since the end of the war. The rate was all-important. To return the Pound to its pre-war value had become the bench-mark of the recovery of Britain's status as the leading world power. Baldwin had established a close friendship with Sir Montagu Norman, Governor of the Bank of England and chief advocate of a return at the pre-war parity. But he was already in the habit of leaving his ministers to take their own decisions and, although he discussed the issue with Churchill, it was in the end up to the Chancellor. By 1925, however, the momentum was almost irresistible. Churchill launched one memorable attack on received wisdom: in a savage memo written from his bed one Sunday morning, he demanded of the Governor of the Bank of England why he 'allows himself to be perfectly happy in the spectacle of Britain possessing the finest credit in the world simultaneously with a million and a quarter unemployed ... I would rather see Finance less proud and Industry more content.'[3] Nonetheless, in his first Budget, on 28 April, he announced that the Pound would return to the gold standard at pre-war parity.

One of the attractions of putting Churchill in the Treasury, Baldwin confided in a private letter, was that he would not be able to talk about Labour. *I do not think Churchill understands the post-war mind ... it's no use just denouncing Socialism as he does. You have got to have an alternative.*[4] Socialism, which few troubled to distinguish from Communism, was a continuing matter of concern. In 1925, half a million men were involved in 600 different industrial disputes. Baldwin was being warned of Soviet funding of extreme left and Communist groupings within some unions. Ramsay MacDonald had twice been forced to take emergency powers in the face of threatened transport strikes. To attack the trade unions, whose links with Communism were much exaggerated but deeply felt, was only partly a question of party advantage. Baldwin's message of industrial co-operation as a route to harmony had yet to be absorbed by the bulk of the party where the mood was for legislation to weaken the unions. In early March, a backbencher, David Macquisten, proposed introducing a bill to require members to opt into rather than out of the trade unions' political levy, a move that would have severely diminished Labour's income. There was wide support for the bill in the party. Baldwin, who regarded the Conservative record on anti-union legislation as a prime cause of the loss of working class support, resisted. He convinced first his Cabinet and then, in a speech that came to be his favourite, the whole House of Commons. At its heart was the responsibility of power: *We find ourselves ... in power, in possession of perhaps the greatest majority our Party has ever had and with the general assent of the country. Now how did we get there? It was not by promising to bring this Bill in; it was because, rightly or wrongly, we succeeded in creating an impression throughout the country that we stood for stable Government and for peace in the country between all classes of the community ... Although I know that there are those who work for different ends from most of us in this House, yet there are many in all ranks and all parties who will re-echo my prayer: 'Give peace in our time, O Lord.'*[5] Even Churchill was impressed.

Although I know that there are those who work for different ends from most of us in this House, yet there are many in all ranks and all parties who will re-echo my prayer: 'Give peace in our time, O Lord.'

BALDWIN

'I had no idea he could show such power ... the whole Conservative Party turned round and obeyed without a single mutineer ... I cease to be astonished at anything.'[6]

The previous September, the Trades Union Congress (TUC) had elected left-wingers to senior positions (more moderate leaders having all been recruited to government) and there had been wild talk of strikes to defeat the government. Unemployment was stubbornly high; the strengthening exchange rate after the return to the gold standard lowered the cost of imports and forced down wages. Coal was once again being produced in the Ruhr and export markets which had buoyed up Britain's decrepit mining industry were being lost to this low-cost, high-quality rival source. The working classes were increasingly being organised into large unions amalgamated from dozens of smaller, more local units. The Transport and General Workers and the General and Municipal Boilermakers were founded in 1922 and 1923 respectively.

The largest union of all was the Miners' Federation. Its principle objective was nationalisation. There had been government control during the war, which had allowed the profitable pits to subsidise pay at the growing number of unprofitable ones. But in 1921 Lloyd George rejected the findings of the 1919 Sankey Commission which had been narrowly in favour of some form of nationalisation, and returned the mines to the private sector. The country had come to the brink of a general strike as owners sought, in their traditional manner, to drive down costs by cutting pay. After a lapse during the war, the Triple Alliance of miners, transport workers and railwaymen was recreated. It was prepared for united action in defence of miners' pay. Lloyd George made preparations for a declaration of a state of emergency. Troops were brought back from far-flung corners of the globe. At the last minute, on 'Black Friday', 21 April 1921, the non-mining unions in the Triple Alliance backed down and the miners struck alone. Now another strike loomed, again backed by the Triple Alliance, as mine owners attempted to claw back concessions on pay made in the brief boom produced by the French occupation of the Ruhr. Miners refused to negotiate. 'Not a penny off the pay, not a minute on the day' became their intransigent cry. The owners, who matched the union for obstinacy and exceeded them in their inability to co-operate to achieve a viable future for the industry, refused to budge too. Hours before the strike was due to begin, Baldwin and Churchill stepped in with a subsidy that would support pay for six months while a further inquiry into the future of the industry, led by Sir Herbert Samuel, took place.

Once more Baldwin shocked his own party. The return to the gold standard, a powerfully deflationary decision, required not open-handed government but deep cuts in planned spending. Churchill was wielding the axe energetically. Baldwin had only just found a settlement to a bitter dispute with the Admiralty over warships that had nearly split his government. Worse, to a nation primed by the popular press to prepare for a war with the workers, it looked like capitulation. To the trade unions it was 'Red Friday', a restoration of power after the betrayal of 'Black Friday' four years earlier. But few thought it anything more than a delay before a confrontation that might lead to revolution. There was widespread sympathy for the miners, victims of an economic juggernaut, Keynes wrote in his denunciation of the return to the gold standard, 'The Economic Consequences of Mr Churchill'. 'If miners were free to transfer themselves to other industries, if a collier out of work … could offer himself as a baker, a bricklayer, or a railway porter at a lower wage … it would be another matter. But notoriously they are not so free. Like other victims of economic transition in past times, the miners are to be offered a choice between starvation and submission, the fruits of their submission to accrue to the benefit of other classes …'[7]

Baldwin sought harmony, but he did not believe that it was government's job to achieve it, only to create the conditions in which it could occur. The return to gold was a long-term measure intended to restore international trade. The short-term cost was a severe squeeze. He denied saying, as the miners alleged, that every worker would have to face a cut in wages to put industry on its feet. But that was the unavoidable implication of his economic policy. He preferred to dwell on his determination to break the reliance of both sides of the coal industry on government to settle their disputes. *The organisations of employers and men … are far more able to work out the solutions of their troubles than the politicians. Let them put the State out of their minds,*[8] he exhorted less than a week before announcing the subsidy. Privately, he wrote: *I may say that we think* [both sides] *are equally stupid and equally bigoted.*[9] Later, he and Churchill justified the subsidy as a way of creating time – time to educate the public about the nature of the dispute, time to prepare for the defence of the State.

For as far as Baldwin was concerned a general strike was a constitutional affront, an attempt to put the interests of one group of citizens above the institution that represented the country as a whole. The Beaverbrook and Rothermere newspapers presented it more simply. It was an attempt at revolution, a challenge that was to be defeated by any means available. Discreetly, the emergency provisions had been in a state of preparedness since 1923. With little success, Communists tried to organise Workers' Defence Corps while MI5 agents intercepted mail and eavesdropped from under platforms. Openly, quasi-Fascist volunteers set up an Organisation for the Maintenance of Supply to prepare for the struggle. The government held it at arm's length, for fear civil unrest might erupt between extremes of left and right independently of the strike. As the months passed, the red scares grew daily more frequent. Little effort was made to bring a sense of proportion to events. The right winger William Joynson-Hicks, Home Secretary, *carrying 200lb of steam to the square inch till every rivet in him is strained to the uttermost*,[10] allowed wildly inaccurate reports of imminent arrests and deportations to go uncorrected. In October, a dozen prominent Communists were locked up for between six and 12 months on blatantly political charges.

On 6 March 1926, Sir Herbert Samuel submitted his report on the coal industry. It was barely eight weeks before the subsidy expired, at which point the owners would shut down the pits and lock out the miners until they were prepared to accept the pay cuts. The Samuel report made no appreciable difference to the position taken by either owners or miners. After some weeks, Baldwin initiated talks with both sides. But he refused to endorse the report, or to guarantee the necessary legislation and funding needed for rationalisation of the industry. The talks, in which Baldwin was observed to find the owners more congenial than the workers, made little progress. On Friday 30 April, as the lockout began, trade union delegates gathered in London to approve the order for a general strike. In Downing Street, the talks, now taken over by a TUC committee, inched ahead. On Saturday 1 May, the TUC delegates approved a general strike but also endorsed the continuation of talks until the final deadline, midnight on 2/3 May. The miners' leaders immediately departed to their various communities. As a result, when the trade union negotiators thought they had a deal to put to them, they were unavailable. By the time enough had returned to London to negotiate, Baldwin was in trouble with his own Cabinet. Ministers had rebelled at the terms he had agreed with the TUC and, threatened with mass resignations, he was forced to withdraw them. The strike began as scheduled 24 hours later.

To Baldwin personally, this was a failure almost as catastrophic as the election defeat of 1923. He did not want the strike. As he told the Commons hours before it began, *I have worked for two years to the utmost of my ability in one direction. I have failed so far. Everything that I care for is being smashed to bits at this moment. That does not take away from me either my faith or my courage.*[11] He could not have gone further to avoid it without splitting his government. However, had he acted earlier, had he enforced mergers and rationalisation to ensure at least parity of sacrifice between owners and workers, and used state aid to develop domestic markets for coal as the more enterprising owners like Sir Alfred Mond were proposing, a strike might have been averted. But Baldwin was determined the govern-

Everything that I care for is being smashed to bits at this moment. That does not take away from me either my faith or my courage.

BALDWIN

ment should never again dabble in an industry's industrial relations. The Party and the Press were eager for a showdown. The TUC dared not abandon the miners again. And neither miners nor their employers would negotiate.

The state was well prepared for self-defence: under the Emergency Powers Act, for six months, the regional authorities had been stockpiling supplies, identifying volunteers and planning for a total shutdown of the economy that in fact did not happen. They were helped by the attitude of the TUC. Union leaders had resolved to bring their members out in waves, beginning with heavy industry and avoiding at all costs cutting off food supplies. As a result, apart from an absence of public transport, in many parts of Britain there was little evidence of the crisis. Most trade unionists saw the strike as a great sympathetic exercise in support of the miners, and were as interested as the government in lowering the temperature and avoiding confrontation. The TUC's first instruction was 'to keep everybody smiling'. They were as anxious as the government that Communists did not provoke violence. They attempted to maintain rigid central control but their organisation was more haphazard and very much less well funded than the government's.

Baldwin sat quietly with Lucy in the Downing Street drawing room with the lights off to save power. Churchill had been given the government propaganda sheet, the *British Gazette*, to run. With enormous energy and at huge cost, he created a newspaper with a print run of over a million, confiscating newsprint, requisitioning warehouses and writing thousands of words of copy aimed at portraying the strike as an incipient revolution. To the bewilderment of most Londoners, he insisted on armed protection for food convoys from the East End docks. Troops were billeted in the Royal Parks and carried out ostentatious military exercises.

Eventually, at the apparent granting of licence to troops to fire on unarmed strikers, even the King remonstrated, also blocking a Treasury move to confiscate trade unions' assets and prevent them paying strike pay to their members.

On the fifth day of the strike, Baldwin made a radio broadcast in which he argued in moderate tones for the defence of the constitution and expressed his willingness to help find a settlement the moment the strike was abandoned. This triggered contacts between the inquiry chairman, Samuel, and the trade unions. By the second Wednesday of the strike they had agreed a form of words that the TUC negotiators persuaded themselves could be presented as a partial triumph. It involved a temporary pay cut, however, and once again the miners refused to accept it, pre-empting the government response and enabling Baldwin to claim a total victory. He used the restoration of popular adulation that followed to insist that the return to work should not be marred by victimisation, an edict largely ignored by the train companies and the dock employers.[12] At the end of the week, Baldwin presented his own plan to resolve the miners' dispute that incorporated some of what the TUC had put forward. It was rejected by both sides.

The General Strike was a catharsis in Britain's industrial relations. Revolution had been averted and having been so real a threat, almost immediately receded out of the public mind. For those millions of middle-class households that had opposed the strike, there was a feeling of national unity more commonly associated with wartime. To them, Baldwin's reputation as a healer was beyond dispute. For five million trade unionists, the immediate future was bleak. Many unions were left on the edge of bankruptcy. Wages continued to fall and unemployment remained around 1.5 million. The number of strikes fell dramatically, although, as trade unions slowly became more professional in their negotiating techniques, a more co-operative approach to industrial relations began to develop. The miners stayed on strike. The owners were now confident of ultimate victory. They had no interest in negotiating and Baldwin had little energy for pursuing it. He also lost the appetite to resist his party's vengeful instincts. He gave in to the owners' demand to restore the eight hour day to the pits. He gave in to the back-bench demand to end contracting-out of the political levy. He resisted all attempts by outside parties, like the Church, to settle the miners' strike, despite the evident hardship endured by the wives and children, reduced in some cases almost to starvation.

Through the summer, Baldwin almost certainly believed the miners would soon settle, as they had in 1921. He despaired of negotiating with Arthur Cook, the miners' secretary, and their president Herbert Smith. In July he told the churchmen who pressed him to intervene *The frightfully difficult task I have to do is to wean this great industry from the breast of the State, where it has been for ten years, and until that industry is on its own feet, we shall have this recurring over and over again ...*[13] At the end of August he overrode the King's request that he stay in the country and retreated to Aix for a complete rest. He crossed the Channel, he reported when he wrote to thank the King for granting permission for him to go, with members of the TUC, with whom he had a *most friendly conversation.* From Aix he kept a close eye on efforts by Churchill, back in London, to resolve the dispute. By letter and telegram he reiterated his determination that no settlement (which for a few days seemed close) could be permitted that perpetuated the involvement of the state. *So long as government can be indicated as a partner so long is there a peg for nationalisation and all the dreams the wild men stand for.*[14]

Baldwin has been criticised, particularly by Roy Jenkins in

his elegant study, for his narrow understanding of the dispute as an outbreak of the endemic ill-feeling between masters and men. Jenkins chastises him for failing to consider the strategic problems of an ageing and uncompetitive industry. But Jenkins betrays the prejudices of a Welsh miner's son.[15] Baldwin knew some mines were unviable. He was prepared to subsidise reorganisation. But neither miners nor owners would consider it. Baldwin saw no justification for giving one industry more help than any other. Iron and steel and shipbuilding had all been severely hit by recession, with many thousands out of work and thousands more taking wage cuts and working on short time. It was unstated government policy – and economic orthodoxy – that as old jobs went, new ones would be created in new industries. By the 1930s, car production lines and domestic consumables like wirelesses and washing machines had begun to create new jobs. Baldwin can be criticised for failing either to consider, or to canvas for, novel ways of government support. But nor did Churchill, that most creative of politicians. It was not until the end of the decade when there were still more than a million unemployed, that intervention was considered. Until then, unemployment was something to be palliated, through public works like the creation of the National Grid and investment in the road network, until trading conditions and the economy improved.

Baldwin's stubbornness in sticking to particular policies that he thought morally necessary was reflected elsewhere. One of his objectives in his determination to clean up after Lloyd George was to restore merit to the honours system, which had come to represent all that was corrupt in the coalition. Legislation establishing an Honours Scrutiny Committee and outlawing the sale of honours was passed in 1925. But Baldwin's private correspondence contains several letters from postulants for honours that demonstrates his resistance. Politely distancing himself from a plea from the notorious political hostess Lady Londonderry, he wrote in December 1924, *Honours always worry me: they have been so flung about the last ten years that it takes a Herculean effort to restore them to something like their old position. I want to make them worth having ...*[16] Even such eminences as the industrialist Sir Alfred Mond, anxious to be elevated to the peerage as a viscount after his recent conversion to the Conservative party, had to be fended off. Mond wrote pressing his case in June 1926. In November that year, the Political Honours Scrutiny Committee objected on the grounds of a recent business deal. It was a further two years before he was finally appointed Baron Melchett. In 1928 Baldwin, who had just learnt of a valuable pearl necklace being sent to Downing Street in payment for a knighthood, was still protesting angrily at the way the system had been milked under Lloyd George. Morality in public life could stand neither the corruption of employing public money to prop up failing industry nor the private party benefit of selling honours.

Honours always worry me: they have been so flung about the last ten years that it takes a Herculean effort to restore them to something like their old position.

BALDWIN

As autumn came, the miners began to return to work. The men went back first in the most prosperous Nottinghamshire coal fields, where a breakaway union was formed, a pattern repeated in the 1983–4 miners' strike. Not until December did the Miners' Federation formally settle, on terms far worse than those available before the strike began. For generations, working-class politics were scarred by a sense of betrayal. Nationally, however, there was a new sense of common purpose and its hero was Stanley Baldwin.

Chapter 5: Disaster (1926–31)

When the General Strike ended on 12 May 1926, Baldwin was mobbed as he left Downing Street for Parliament, cheered in the House of Commons and thanked by his united Cabinet. He reached a peak of personal popularity that a different politician might have used to stamp his character more firmly on the party, or his party on the country. Baldwin had another concept of leadership. A *magnificent opportunity for service* he had called his 1924 election landslide. The service he most wished to perform was to educate the country's new democracy in Conservative values. The Victorians had called it 'Government by speaking', an idea Baldwin took for his own. *We have to see that the heart of the Empire is sound and to that we must educate and educate and educate,*[2] he told a party gathering in 1924. He wanted to achieve *the spiritual sanitation of our people*, a climate where moral values might flourish, a world as he said to the Junior Imperial League in March 1928, not so much safe for democracy, but where democracy was safe for the world.

Peace and Faith your Creed,
Stanley Boy!
True in Word and Deed,
Stanley Boy!
Socialist will hamper,
Lloyd George prove a damper,
In our hours of need.
Stanley Boy![1]

Under its broad umbrella, the Conservative Party retained

in uneasy fellowship Tory die-hard knights of the shires, low-tax suburban and city types and raving anti-socialists. Baldwin had to fashion a different kind of Conservatism that, without doing violence to the sentiments of any of its core supporters, would appeal to a wider audience and respond to the new mood of idealism that fuelled the Labour Party. Tories too were people who dreamed dreams and were committed to the betterment of the people. This message he carried around the country. He made more speeches to a wider range of audiences than is conventional for a prime minister, on subjects that were not exclusively and sometimes not at all political. He spoke often of the duties of citizenship and democracy, of friendship, of England and English traditions, classic writers and the countryside. He described himself as a master of platitudes. The deputy Cabinet Secretary, Tom Jones, who had become a close friend, thought he appealed to 'the eternal commonplaces'.

Speech-making had not come easily to him and an important occasion still required days of effort. *I just want a quiet morning to think*, he wrote to Mimi Davidson. *It is just that getting two or three hours undisturbed, walking about the room and sitting in an armchair that restores my equilibrium. It is by turning over things in my mind that the precipitate is formed out of which the speeches come and if I don't go through that curious preparatory cud-chewing, then the work suffers …*[3]

Baldwin considered rhetoric dishonest but his use of language and his understanding of the power of words made him an often brilliant public speaker. He enjoyed the contact with the audience (complaining bitterly when technological advance introduced microphones to mass meetings). For the new medium of broadcasting, he mastered a quite different, more intimate approach. He understood quickly that he was speaking to people in their own homes and used not a script but a few headings on a scrap of paper. 'Watching him in action, I am sure a manuscript would have bothered and not helped him,' a BBC veteran recalled. 'He spoke somewhat slowly and deliberately ... made no gestures with his hands, and remained all the time looking directly at the microphone, as though engaged in earnest conversation with a man immediately opposite him in the room.'[4]

The day-to-day routine of government seemed almost an intrusion on this larger mission. By 1927, there was a sense of an administration already spent. Advisers like Geoffrey Dawson of the *Times* pressed Baldwin to reshuffle his Cabinet where characters familiar from decades in public life stagnated for the full duration of the government. He set out the difficulties of change to one supplicant for office: *He pleases one: he cannot please more than one: he may hurt some. He has, with due regard to the best interest of the country, to make such a selection as will accommodate itself best to the health and well-being of the large party of which he is for the time being leader. And in that he must rely largely – certainly finally – on his best judgement by which ultimately he must stand or fall.*[5] In Baldwin's governments, alteration came only in the face of death, illness or poverty.

Some ministers made good use of this stability. As Health Minister, Neville Chamberlain's remit covered housing, local government and pensions as well as health itself. He managed to get 23 of the 25 bills he had planned onto the statute book. Measures were introduced to speed up slum clearance. Contributory pensions were improved and extended, and far-reaching reforms of local government were brought in to which Churchill, from the Treasury, added a new system of finance that went a little way to compensating poorer boroughs, which had to find resources to meet higher welfare burdens. There was some effort to ease unemployment through useful developments of the national infrastructure, notably the Electricity Supply Act that established the National Grid, a public body run by a government-appointed management board. The BBC, not only because of its helpful attitude during the General Strike, was awarded Corporation status, thus preserving it as a public service rather than – as some in the party preferred – allowing the new medium to be developed commercially. Curiously, the most right-wing of Home Secretaries, Joynson-Hicks, piloted through legislation in honour of an election pledge to give women the vote at 21, completing the introduction of universal adult suffrage.

At the Treasury, Churchill maintained a tight control of expenditure that led to severe cuts in planned defence spending. Lloyd George's 'Ten Year Rule', the assumption that Britain would be involved in no major war for the next decade, was applied with dire consequences for future military capacity and consequently for diplomacy. When Baldwin remonstrated on particular issues like the cancellation of improvements to the naval base at Singapore (where he got his way), he was warned that it was either the guns of imperial defence or the butter of social reform. Disarmament and the League of Nations were, it was almost universally hoped, the way ahead. The US, Britain and Japan tried (but failed) to agree on the respective sizes of their navies. The Locarno Treaty of 1925 guaranteed France and Germany's common frontiers, although its provision to fight first and consult later offended the Dominions who were reluctant to be committed to another European war. The status of the

> **Baldwin** had only discovered the reality of working-class housing in 1925 in Dundee. *We first visited some slum houses. I never saw such a sight. Oddly enough I had never been in real slum houses, and I as near as two pins sat down and howled: the whole thing came to me with such force. Five and six in one room. Think of the children!*[6]

Dominions themselves was to be set out in law following the 1926 Imperial Conference, changes that were embodied in the Statute of Westminster in 1931. War itself, at least aggressive war, was outlawed by the Kellogg-Briand Pact. At the League of Nations in Geneva, diplomats began hesitantly to learn the language of international co-operation and collective security.

It was a period of slow, incremental change, 'Tory socialism' Charles Loch Mowat called it in his definitive account of the period, *Britain between the Wars*.[7] Baldwin felt it had been the most productive session since 1906. It brought in the kind of moderate change the voters thought they wanted in 1924 and which Baldwin saw as the necessary background for the entrenching of responsible mass democracy. He continued to shy away from confrontation, and he disliked it as much in the cabinet room as in the country. The public knew it from the way he smothered plans to reform the House of Lords after the rejection of the original proposals, which would have made Conservative power in the upper house invulnerable. His ministers knew it from his long silences in Cabinet, where he listened as his ministers argued, weighing in only in the last resort. He expected ministers to get on with running their departments on their own. He was always available for conversation, but he would not take their decisions for them. He was more likely to write facetious notes to colleagues than to discuss policy detail with them. He was generous in encouraging ministers to take the holidays that he so relied on himself. A letter to his Home Secretary, Joynson-Hicks, in January 1928 gives a flavour of his genial style and relaxed approach: *Now do be sensible. We shall have practically settled our programme* [before you come back] *... there can be nothing for which you are needed (I say 'needed' because you are always wanted by your friends) until the House meets ... You will have a heavy year* *in any circumstances. And now that you have taken the Protestants of England under your wing* [On his own account, Joynson-Hicks was fighting attempts to revise the Book of Common Prayer] *as well as the police, the publicans, the prisoners, the prostitutes, factories, flappers and children, you MUST learn to take* [care] *of yourself, or all the above will be ORPHANED. Now just think this over. I don't want to see you till the sixth of February.*[8]

In the party there were rumblings of discontent, only partially assuaged by sporadic activity like the Trade Disputes Act or, in May 1927 in a final flare of anti-Communism, the Arcos raid, where a Special Branch sweep of the Anglo-Russian trading company produced mountains of paper but not the alleged target, a single subversive document. The party malcontents, however, had no rival around whom they could gather. Baldwin himself, contemplating the succession in 1927, ruled out Churchill as unacceptable to the party, while his own close friend Lord Irwin was in India as Viceroy. Baldwin preferred the Lord Chancellor,

Edward Wood (1881–1959), had a confusing number of identities. He became Lord Irwin in 1925, and the 3rd Viscount Halifax in 1934. He was a reforming Viceroy of India from 1925–31 and then attached to the Foreign Office from 1935 to 1940 when, to his distress, he nearly became prime minister instead of Churchill. He was a successful ambassador in Washington from 1941–6. He was also a Fellow of All Souls, and Chancellor of Oxford University from 1933 to 1959.

Lord Hailsham, but thought the choice would come to rest with Neville Chamberlain. But Baldwin was in no hurry to retire, unless forced to by his continually worsening financial position. He relied heavily on income from the family firm, and like all heavy industry in the 1920s it was producing no dividends. When he lost Downing Street, he had to rely on the Duke of Westminster to find him a house at a peppercorn rent in central London.

On 30 May 1929, after a campaign built around the steady, unassuming personality of the Prime Minister under the slogan 'Safety First', Baldwin went to the country. He was confident of the result, he had told Ramsay MacDonald at a meeting to discuss the new parliament a few weeks earlier. But it was Labour that emerged, for the first time, as the largest party. Once again there was a hung parliament. With Lloyd George leading the Liberals, there was no question of a coalition under Baldwin's leadership. Baldwin resigned as Prime Minister almost immediately to let Labour once more form a minority government. Stamfordham relayed his thinking to the King. 'He has been beaten and in the true English spirit he accepts his defeat and, if he resigns, the Democracy in an equally British spirit will take off their hats to him as a good sportsman.'[9] This, Baldwin anticipated, would be remembered at the next election, which was unlikely to be far away.

Baldwin blamed the Liberals for the defeat. The Conservatives had won more votes than at the last election, and more votes than Labour at this one. But nearly 200 more Liberals had fought seats and they had attracted a healthy 28 per cent of the vote, only ten per cent behind both Labour and Conservative, for a mere 59 seats. When he lost his seat in 1924, Asquith had retired to the Lords. Lloyd George, after disagreeing with the party's largely pro-government line during the General Strike, had returned to the political fold and under his leadership the party had produced the most original responses to the continuing economic and industrial crises. The Liberal 'Yellow Book', as its programme 'Britain's Industrial Future' was dubbed, was published in 1928 with proposals for new structures for industrial relations, public control of national concerns, improved economic information for government, and above all an extensive programme of public works to modernise Britain's transport infrastructure, to be financed by borrowing. 'We can beat unemployment', Lloyd George's campaign slogan said, and he claimed that within a year the numbers of jobless could be reduced to 'normal' levels, for creating jobs directly for 350,000 people would create twice as many more by reviving domestic consumption. Whitehall told Baldwin it could not be done. To the electorate, Baldwin responded with a dissertation on Lloyd George's record, warning voters not to be misled by *specious promises* and begging them to choose on the basis of *fact not fable*. But people wanted reassurance that government could do something, and Baldwin had no ideas to offer, putting his faith in valuable but too modest expansions of state education, and mother and child welfare. Protection remained too contentious an idea to be advanced and the idea of some kind of empire trading system, he rejected. The landowners' and farmers' plea for safeguards to protect them from the worst agricultural depression in 50 years raised the unacceptable spectre of dear food and was rejected.

In his conversation with MacDonald before the election, Baldwin had acknowledged that he was no good as leader of the opposition. He knew that his distaste for what MacDonald called 'the old noisy political sham fights', and his natural instinct for fair play, left his party discontented. Even so, he cannot have anticipated the grim struggle that nearly engulfed him over the following two years.

It was partly circumstance; having lost more than 200 seats and with them some of the 'YMCA', the brightest and best of the young MPs like Harold Macmillan and Duff Cooper, the rump of the party at Westminster was disproportionately influenced by the imperially-minded diehard tendency from the Home Counties, with whom Baldwin, thinking of the marginal seats he must win back in the North, was unavoidably at loggerheads. Partly it was events: the India Commission that Baldwin himself had set up under the Liberal jurist Sir John Simon was contemplating Dominion status for the 'jewel in the crown' of the Empire. Lord Irwin, on leave in London from the vice regal palace, pressed the merits of Home Rule and warned of violence if no move was made. The diehards, led at the gallop by Winston Churchill, prepared to resist. Sacrificing a leader of whom they were anyway deeply suspicious would be no disincentive. And partly, it was Baldwin's own reluctance to pay attention to policy development which left a gap at the heart of the party's appeal, one that Lord Beaverbrook was only to happy to fill with another campaign, this one for Empire Free Trade, that might end in unseating Baldwin. When India and Empire Free Trade collided, Baldwin's career hung by the slender thread of a single by-election.

I shall take a long holiday this autumn, Baldwin wrote in June to his son Oliver, now a Labour MP. *I can't leave my party in the hour of defeat.... I am fortunately so constituted that party triumphs or disasters do not unduly affect me, and my soul is quietly content.*[10] Apart from the nine months in 1924, the Conservative party had not been in opposition since the early years of the war 15 years earlier. There was much on which to reflect. The party, faced with Labour again on the government benches, was restless. It recognised that Baldwin was a great electoral asset. But that could not make them love him, nor his liberal tendencies. In July Beaverbrook, who used his *Daily Express* almost exclusively as a weapon of political influence, took up what he termed a 'Crusade' (the Crusader is still on the *Express* masthead) for Empire Free Trade – literally, creating a free trade zone throughout the empire, protected by a tariff wall. Its early progress was handicapped by the weakness that the Dominions already operated tariffs and were not necessarily enthusiasts for the scheme, while food taxes in Britain had a lamentable electoral record. But by the following year Beaverbrook had gained enough support for Baldwin to feel it necessary to commit the party once more to a degree of safeguarding and protection, although he refused to contemplate tariffs on wheat and meat. Beaverbrook raised the stakes by launching a United Empire Party, backed by his fellow press baron Lord Rothermere, which immediately attracted more than a hundred thousand supporters. *I am fighting with beasts at Ephesus*, Baldwin wrote to Sir John Simon, *and I hope to see their teeth drawn and their claws broken before the battle is over*![11] But Beaverbrook was not easily deterred and he was intent on changing the party's policy. The attacks resumed. Baldwin, pleading once more the need to educate the electorate, conceded a referendum on food taxes and, showing a subtlety of manoeuvre that might have surprised his public, gently eased Beaverbrook – for whom he had some affection – and Rothermere – whom he detested – apart. By midsummer 1930, the feeling against the leadership had focused on Baldwin's close ally, J C C Davidson, party chairman and author of the 1929 election campaign, and as Baldwin sadly acknowledged in a consoling letter on his resignation, an obvious surrogate for the leader himself. In Davidson's place, Neville Chamberlain became chairman, a post for which he had manoeuvred as base camp for a leadership bid. But although by this move, he became Baldwin's natural successor, he would be damaged if he was forced from office. Baldwin would have to choose his time of departure. At a memorable speech at Caxton Hall called to rally support on 24 June, Baldwin turned on his persecutors with one of the orations he seemed best able to produce when under the greatest pressure. *I like the other man to begin the fight and then I am ready. When I fight, I go on to the end*, he warned. Then he produced an extraordinary letter from Lord Rothermere demanding, in return for the support of his newspapers, approval for the bulk of a future Baldwin cabinet and the principle policies it would pursue. This, Baldwin declared, was no more than the kind of pressure the TUC had tried to exert in the General Strike. *A more preposterous and insolent demand was never made on the leader of any political party. I repudiate it with contempt and I will fight that attempt at domination to the end.*

Baldwin had rescued himself; but he had not stopped the campaign for Empire Free Trade that Conservative by-election candidates were now facing wherever they stood. The tension was heightened by the imminence of a new Imperial Confer-ence that would be gathering in the autumn at which the whole idea could be discussed. While the Baldwins were recu-perating from the year's exertions in Aix, the mood worsened. Nervous constituency chairmen reported surging support for the Beaverbrook campaign. When Baldwin returned home, he was persuaded to call another party meeting to shore up – or finally destroy – his position. But at the Imperial Con-ference, Dominion Prime Ministers opened up the debate on protection and, pushed by Chamberlain, Baldwin rewrote party policy in a single statement that came out in support of Imperial preference without recourse to referendum or election. The question about food taxes, on which Churchill made it clear he would resign, was left blurred. At the same time, a by-election in South Paddington looked likely to go to the United Empire Party. The Party meeting was set for polling day. *I have rubbed the seat of my breeches with cobblers' wax as a precaution ...*, he wrote cheerily to Davidson. As he arrived at Caxton Hall, on the far side of Parliament Square from the Palace of Westminster, he encouraged the photographers to take their pictures now, *It may be the last time you see me*. In fact, he secured an overwhelming victory, by 462 to 116, among the Conservative peers and MPs who controlled his fate. Even the King of Lancashire, Lord Derby, who had told him before the meeting that he thought he would have to resign, wrote afterwards that now he would do all that he could to support him.

The tariff question was essentially a party matter, at least as much about Baldwin's style of leadership as the relevance of tariffs as a response to economic crisis.[12] Securing a democratic, self-governing India was of a different order, scope for what G.M. Young called 'the final achievement of English political genius.' Influenced by perhaps his closest political friend, Lord Irwin, Baldwin knew the outcome he wanted – Dominion status – and he intended to achieve it regardless of opposition from the party's right wing which made him *feel the hopelessness of trying to liberalise the Tory party* ...[13] In June 1930, as Baldwin fought off the Press Barons, the Simon Commission reported against the immediate granting of Dominion status, while in India Gandhi led a campaign of civil disobedience resulting in hundreds of thousands of arrests. The Tory Party's instinctive response to civil unrest was the smack of firm government and an end to what they saw as appeasement. Instead Baldwin supported MacDonald's proposal for a round-table conference that, although boycotted by Congress politicians, met in London in the autumn of 1930, for the first stage of drafting a new constitution for an All-India Federation. Churchill, who had been unhappy about protection, was inflamed at his party's India policy and reverted (in Baldwin's eyes) to the subaltern of Hussars, '96, denouncing concessions to nationalism that would lead to the severance of all ties between Britain and India as 'a hideous act of self-mutilation'. In January, he resigned from

Baldwin's shadow cabinet. He did not return to government until 1939.

Churchill was a powerful inspiration to the malcontents. Over the next six weeks, Baldwin's position deteriorated sharply as India and Empire Free Trade merged to create an impression of a divided and unhappy party whose leader would take it only in a direction it did not want to go. At the beginning of March, Neville Chamberlain showed Baldwin a memorandum illustrating the degree to which the party in the country had lost confidence in him. His initial reaction was to resign at once. Chamberlain would be his anointed successor. Friends swiftly changed his mind. Another by-election was pending, in the heart of the most expensive and fashionable part of London, the St George's division of Westminster. The press barons were running an Empire Free Trade candidate and the Conservative candidate, refusing to defend Baldwin, had resigned in his favour. In a moment of Quixotic romanticism, Baldwin toyed with the idea of resigning his own seat and standing himself. At the eleventh hour, Duff Cooper agreed to fight for the Conservatives, and Baldwin learnt that the memorandum of party morale was based more on supposition than fact. But his recovery faltered when he mishandled a back-bench attempt to bounce him into withdrawing support for the next round table conference on India. However he had decided that, unlike the press barons' campaign for Empire

Sir John Simon, the Liberal jurist, had been asked by Baldwin in 1927 to determine India's future development. In June 1930 the Commission recommended the establishment of 'responsible government' in the Indian provinces – which were ruled by the princes – and further negotiations between British India, the British government and the princes about the future of the central government.

Free Trade, India was an issue of principle on which he could be proud to be defeated. Now deep into the last ditch, on 12 March 1931 he produced another memorable speech defending his determination to maintain cross-party unity on India's future, the inevitability of accommodating change in the Empire, and the need for party leaders to tell their followers the truth, 'because truth is greater than tactics'. Internally, it was a triumph. Outside, the press barons persisted. 'A vote for Duff Cooper is a vote for Ghandi' [*sic*], the headlines shouted. Five days after his Commons triumph and two days before polling day in St George's, Baldwin excoriated the press barons in terms still vivid: *What the proprietors are aiming at is power, and power without responsibility — the prerogative of the harlot throughout the ages.* Duff Cooper won the by-election. But Baldwin's problems lingered. He conceded protection for agriculture. But only a general election would save him.

What the proprietors are aiming at is power, and power without responsibility — the prerogative of the harlot throughout the ages.

BALDWIN

Chapter 6: Worn-out Tools (1931–7)

History levels two charges against Stanley Baldwin: a lack of imagination in dealing with the slump and its aftermath, and a lack of energy in responding to the threat of Hitler. To these Roy Jenkins has added a third – that, through over-reaction to what Jenkins (with the eye of an ex-Chancellor who had seen off a number of major financial crises himself) thought a 'relatively minor' financial crisis, he threw away all his success in rebuilding the two-party system around a respectable Labour Party and a modernised Conservative Party. Instead he was founder and mainstay of a monolithic national government that, lacking a significant opposition in Parliament, was overly influenced by extra-parliamentary expressions of opinion and particularly the mood of pacifism among the electorate.[1]

Well, they've got into this mess, let them get out of it.

BALDWIN

In the second half of his years at the summit of British politics, from 1931–7, Baldwin had to deal at the same time with three crises any one of which would have been a major political test. He was faced with a minority Labour government that had yet to reconcile its utopian ambitions with its democratic convictions. He had to deal with national and international financial crisis. He had to deal with the ambitions of the dictators thrown up by the aftermath of war, revolution and economic collapse.

For the first time, but not the last, an incoming Labour government had to handle an inherited financial disaster. The 1929 election had been held in a mood of mild optimism. During the summer, unemployment fell slightly. But in October came the Wall Street Crash. Any prospect of recovery vanished as finance got the jitters and international trade seized-up. In January 1930, the jobless total had remained steady at 1.5 million, but it was 2 million in July and 2.5 million in December. The rate of increase slowed, but a year later the total was 3 million. It did not fall below 2 million until 1938. For the minority Labour government whose finances were in the control of the rigorously orthodox Philip Snowden, what turned out to be the worst of many consequences was the level of borrowing required to support what was supposed to be a self-financing scheme of unemployment insurance. In early 1931, Sir George May was invited to examine ways of making economies. That summer, first the Austrian and then the German central banks went into meltdown. On 31 July, the May report was published, warning of a £120 million budget deficit and calling for a balanced budget to be achieved by raising taxes and cutting expenditure, particularly on unemployment benefit. For a report intended to avert disaster, it was remarkably successful in precipitating it. The bankers, already deserting sterling, lacked confidence in the Labour government's will to make the cuts May recommended. There was a dramatic run on gold.

MacDonald, whose absence of faith in his colleagues was amply returned – Baldwin had recently revealed to him that a Labour back-bencher had asked for his advice on unseating a prime minister – broke off his holiday in Lossiemouth. Baldwin, motoring out to Aix, also broke off his journey and returned to London. He, MacDonald and Sir Herbert Samuel (standing in as Liberal leader for Lloyd George who was recuperating from illness) met on 13 August. Neville Chamberlain, also at the meeting and perhaps still frustrated from coming so near to replacing Baldwin earlier in the year, reported that Baldwin said nothing constructive and appeared anxious to resume his holiday, which he did that evening. Baldwin, it was later reported by one leading banker, was determined that Labour bear the responsibility for the crisis.[2] The subject for discussion at the meeting was the willingness of the opposition leaders to support MacDonald's efforts to stabilise the situation. He had not entirely abandoned hope of persuading his cabinet to accept the cuts; but he cannot have been optimistic. All-party support would reassure foreign creditors of his serious intent, but more probably he would need it in the face of internal opposition to the solutions he believed unavoidable. He wanted the Opposition's backing while his Cabinet economics sub-committee decided where the axe should fall. When Cabinet met to debate the committee's recommendations, MacDonald and Snowden were already determined that the cuts were large enough and in a form to be acceptable to the other parties. That meant it was impossible to place the burden of balancing the budget on tax increases rather than spending cuts. Labour ministers would not accept that. MacDonald had chosen the bankers and, he believed, the national interest, over his party.

Informed of the impasse in Cabinet, once more Baldwin interrupted his holiday to return to London. On his way back, he met Davidson in Paris to discuss the options. He had told Chamberlain that he thought it 'all to the good that the government have to look after their own chickens as they come home to roost'. But by 22 August, MacDonald was on the brink of resignation and a devaluation of sterling – the pound being forced off the gold standard – was rumoured, a national humiliation that Baldwin could not allow to happen. From Paris, he wrote to Lucy, *There won't be an Election yet. The urgency of economy is so great that it has to be forced through this House.*[3] [original emphasis]

Talk of a national government had been the stuff of political society gossip for most of the past 18 months, fuelled by the mood of crisis, and magnified through the unflattering prism of the daily newspapers. Obliquely, MacDonald had several times raised the idea with close friends. After the *démarche*, his colleagues remembered events that had had no significance at the time. Sidney Webb had recently received a letter from him saying 'we have not the material in our party that we ought to have'. A year later the remark became the basis for the first of many excoriating articles accusing MacDonald of conspiracy. By August, Chamberlain too was beginning to see a national government as unavoidable and not necessarily undesirable. But Baldwin had specifically ruled it out in a speech in Hull in July 1931, and again on 1 August. He could not support a government that would not introduce tariff reform, and Labour was a free trade party.

When he returned to London early on 23 August it was far from clear that a national government would be among the choices he was required to make. If he could not get the cuts, MacDonald appeared ready to resign with the rest of his Cabinet, forcing the Conservatives to form a government to see the crisis out. Baldwin spent the morning discussing options with the editor of *The Times*, his friend Geoffrey Dawson, and only learnt when he called in at his club for lunch that the King wanted to see him. As a result, the King had already seen and been persuaded by Samuel, a lucid enthusiast for coalition, of the case for a national government, under MacDonald (whose presence was needed to make the cuts 'palatable' to the working classes). The King's mind was made up when he and Baldwin met at 3.00 p.m. in the afternoon, and it was then impossible for Baldwin to overrule him. However, Dawson, who had already spoken to the King's private secretary, had also pressed Baldwin to support MacDonald; he should not be allowed to resign. He should be made 'to get the country out of the mess'. 'I thought it was everything to get a plan of national economy put out in public by a Labour Government, since it was the only course that would have a permanent effect in reversing a policy of extravagance.'[4] This would have been a persuasive argument for Baldwin, who recoiled at the prospect of the Conservatives alone carrying the responsibility for cutting the incomes of the poorest in the land. The King's appeal to him to put the national interest before that of party hardly needed to be made.

The drama continued as Sunday 23 August wore on. MacDonald's Cabinet met at 7.00 p.m. More than an hour later they received the long awaited telegram from the government's New York agents in response to the desperate request for a loan of a further £100 million. It could only be arranged, the government was told, if the necessary cuts to balance the budget had already been made. The bankers were determining British domestic policy. By 11 votes to 10, cabinet refused to authorise the cuts. At 10.20 the King interrupted dinner to receive an emotional MacDonald. Downing Street had telephoned ahead to warn that shouts had been heard from the Cabinet room and the Prime Minister was distraught. The King calmed him, persuaded him he was the only man who could lead the country and they agreed to meet again in the morning with Baldwin and Samuel. The following day, it was decided to form a national Emergency Government to pass the necessary economic measures. It would exist with a small cabinet for as short a time as necessary. Thereafter there would be an election at which the parties would fight under their own colours, although the National Government would remain until a new government was formed.

The King was delighted as always by such a display of national unity. He was particularly impressed that Baldwin was prepared to serve under MacDonald. In his turn, Baldwin always paid tribute to MacDonald's courage in leaving his party behind in order to do what he believed right. MacDonald's party took a more jaundiced view. Only three Labour cabinet ministers followed him on his self-proclaimed suicide mission. Baldwin himself, in a very English demonstration of humility, was to be Lord President of the Council, number three in the government behind the Prime Minister and Lord Chancellor. *Politically, we are on velvet*, Baldwin wrote to one friend.[5]

Having constructed a ten-man Cabinet of four Labour, four Conservatives (Neville Chamberlain, Samuel Hoare and Philip Cunliffe-Lister joined Baldwin) and two Liberals, the National Government's first task was to get the cuts through Parliament against the opposition of all but the fifteen Labour MPs prepared to follow MacDonald. But this demonstration of will was not enough to end the financial crisis. Among naval ratings at Invergordon, whose wages were to suffer along with those of other state employees like teachers and civil servants, and of course the jobless recipients of unemployment benefit, there was something approaching what the newspapers called a mutiny. Communist involvement was suspected. A renewed assault on the pound led inexorably to the final crisis on 21 September and the decision to abandon the gold standard: the main purpose of the National Government had been jettisoned. Yet the heavens did not fall. The bulk of the Labour Party which had argued for devaluation turned out to be right.

Sometime between the formation of the National Government, with the express intent of going to the country as individual parties, and the decision to abandon gold, opinion had swung in favour of the National Government staying together to see the recovery through. On the one hand, there was alarm that the main Labour Party was gathering strength from its stand against the cuts and concern that in an election it might reap the advantage among the working classes of promising a return to high spending funded by higher taxes; on the other, reports were coming in from local Conservative parties of a demand to keep politics out of the emergency. *The Times* began to make the case for the election to be fought by the National Government, to secure a mandate for a tariff and tackle the wider issues of a national recovery. This was the kind of advice that Dawson knew would appeal to Baldwin (there is no evidence, however, that they had discussed it). Baldwin's old friend Montagu Norman told him the bankers wanted a big majority on the side of sound finance. But he also understood the extraordinary political opportunity opening in front of him, from which the Conservative Party might emerge as the truly national party. The continued presence of Labour and Liberal ministers would reassure foreign bankers of the national resolve to deal toughly with the economic crisis. But the dominant party would be the Conservatives. The problem now was to find the language to cover the large gaps between the three parties' views of what was required.

Baldwin could not go into an election without an express commitment to a tariff. MacDonald was prepared to reconsider his long opposition, but still hoped to be able to bring Labour's moderates in behind him in a new centre grouping, perhaps with some or all of the Liberal party. That ambition was destroyed when Labour's National Executive summarily expelled him and the ministers who had followed him into the National Government. The bulk of the Liberals were still committed to free trade and wanted to delay an election. As a result Baldwin, who feared losing the Liberals might cost the National Government MacDonald too, gave up the idea of a direct appeal for approval for a tariff, and reverted to a bland expression that had come to the Conservatives' aid before: the National Government should seek a mandate for a 'free hand' to do what was necessary. But it was impossible for the Liberals to agree even to such a non-committal undertaking. Finally it was accepted that the three parties would fight on their own manifestos, but with agreement to work together afterwards. MacDonald, who would continue to serve as Prime Minister after the election, would issue a statement of principle. The outcome would be read as approval for 'a doctor's mandate' – that is, the argument over tariffs was in theory suspended, to be resumed when the electorate had shown its preference.

The result was an overwhelming endorsement for the National Government: votes for its candidates outnumbered its opponents by two to one. But what was a handsome majority of the votes became

Five hundred and fifty-four of the new MPs supported the National Government, against just 61 who opposed it. Of its supporters, the overwhelming number, 473, were Conservatives, although MacDonald and 12 of the 19 other national Labour candidates had achieved spectacular victories. The Liberals, split three ways into tariff supporters under Sir John Simon, free-traders under Sir Herbert Samuel, and a small Lloyd-George family group, were finished for at least the next 70 years.

a crushing and unprecedented landslide in the House of Commons. Labour was left with only 52 MPs, but it had been defeated by a sharp drop in the number of three-way contests.

Its share of the vote fell slightly less disastrously, from 37 per cent to 30.6 per cent.

The Conservatives were left a little dazed. Baldwin, in a note of congratulation to MacDonald, wrote of *this amazing popular mandate*. To Lord Derby, he talked of the country sending out an SOS. Davidson, unwisely but perhaps accurately, wrote 'in effect, we have a dictatorship'. Baldwin was rather more wary about the dangers of such an overwhelming and under-employed majority, not least in sustaining the impression of a government that reflected the interests of the whole country. Government jobs from posts in the Cabinet down to the most junior whips' positions were shared out allowing the Conservatives only a small advantage. Of the 20 posts in MacDonald's first Cabinet, only 11 went to Tories. The most basic tool of party management, patronage, could be used only sparingly. One of the tasks Baldwin wanted to be free to perform as Lord President – and therefore without departmental responsibilities – was to manage the party, and the House of Commons.

A tariff of some form was now widely accepted in the City and industry as the only route out of economic and industrial crisis. Even Liberals like Keynes had been persuaded that free trade was not a precondition of recovery, although that did nothing to weaken the resolve of the Liberals in Cabinet. They remained sceptical that the national governments' objectives – to restore employment, allow industry to rationalise and modernise and international trade to resume – would be served by the national isolationism implied by tariffs, exchange controls and import quotas. But they had no other answer to offer to Britain's unemployment which, by the turn of the year, was touching three million. The pound remained in need of frequent support. Desperate measures were needed and tariff reform seemed more persuasive than inertia. Robert

Skidelsky's magisterial account of Keynes's life paints an alarming picture of the political classes stumped by the crisis, muted by what the economist called the 'business Conservatism' of the new Chancellor of the Exchequer, Neville Chamberlain, together with the submergence of the Liberal party and the lack of influence of the 'old liberal-minded world of clubs and committees, of civil servants and of bankers, politicians and economists and do-gooders ...'.[6] Towards the end of 1931, Keynes began work on 'The General Theory'; but the analysis that was to shape the world's economies after 1945 had hardly taken form in its author's mind. Neville Chamberlain was resolved to fulfil the ambitions that his father Joseph had shared with Baldwin's father Alfred 30 years earlier. Emergency protectionist measures were taken immediately. The Board of Trade, whose President, the Liberal Sir Walter Runciman, had now been recruited to the protectionist cause, launched an inquiry at which only evidence in favour of protection was heard. In January 1932, the government trembled when the free trade Liberals – Samuel, Sir Donald Maclean and Sir Archibald Sinclair – threatened to resign. MacDonald persuaded them the national interest – that is, the survival of the national government – was more important than their free trade principles. At the end of the summer of 1932, Baldwin headed the British delegation to an Imperial Economic Conference that gathered in Canada, where it was hoped some form of preference would be given to goods produced by British industry. However, the Dominions were unwilling to risk jobs in their own infant industries in order to save jobs in Britain, and even with Baldwin's emollient presence, agreement could be reached, not to cut tariffs, but only to raise tariffs against non-Empire imports.

The last argument for tariff reform was fought out in the Commons, between Chamberlain and the Samuelite Liberals, a battle no less edgy for the minority position of the free traders. MacDonald and Baldwin were both anxious to shore up the support structure for the national government by finding a way to keep the free trade Liberals – and Snowden, Privy Seal but now in the Lords – in the government. They had succeeded in January. But in September, the game was up. Snowden wrote bitterly to MacDonald: 'They have sacrificed nothing, but have used the enormous Tory majority we gave them at the Election to carry out a Tory policy and to identify us with it. We have sacrificed our Party and ruined the political careers of a score of young Labour MPs.'[7]

In 1932, President Roosevelt launched his New Deal in the USA. But the idea of carrying out similar extensive programmes of public works was political and economic anathema to Baldwin and Chamberlain: too redolent of Lloyd George, too reminiscent of spendthrift Labour. Later, it could be seen that a recovery was already beginning. September 1932 marked the high tide of unemployment. Interest rates were cut from 6 per cent to 2 per cent; the terms of trade turned in Britain's favour. Commodity prices fell and stayed low. The cost of living fell, but wages for the majority in work did not, and a new domestic, consumption-led market, anticipated by Baldwin ten years earlier, began to replace exports which finally reached 1927 levels by volume in 1936. The unsatisfactory Dominion trading arrangements led to a proliferation of bilateral agreements with European countries, based on the use of tariffs to negotiate favourable terms – a small victory for Baldwin's view that tariffs would paradoxically lead to the liberalisation of trade. There was a shift in the pattern of Britain's trade. Through the decade, trade with the

Empire grew faster than trade with Europe in both imports and exports. The iron and steel industries did make some progress at rationalising, but with painful consequences. The removal of surplus shipbuilding capacity led to the closure of the shipyards at Jarrow in 1932 and a move to build a new steel plant there was vetoed by the new British steel conglomerate. Unemployment in the town reached 80 per cent and in 1936 200 of the unemployed set off for London, led by their MP, Ellen Wilkinson, in the Jarrow March. There were many other 'hunger marches', particularly from South Wales where the coal industry remained in severe depression, squeezed out of its European markets by German coal. The mine owners, as obstinate as they had been during the strike in 1926, refused to rationalise and obstructed government's insufficiently determined attempts to compel reorganisation.

For empirical rather than ideological reasons, however, Conservative thinking began to favour state intervention. Although it was not until 1938 that the government finally nationalised mineral royalties, a move that paved the way to coal nationalisation in 1946. In 1931, the national government rescued Herbert Morrison's plans for a London Passenger Transport board to control tubes, buses and trams in the capital and to expand and modernise services. Neville Chamberlain used a return to budget surplus in 1934 to sponsor a great wave of house building. He also introduced Special Area Status, to try to encourage new industry into the most depressed parts of Britain. Unfortunately, what was remembered most vividly was the introduction of the means test. Unemployed Assistance Boards, independent of local government and funded by the Treasury, were introduced in 1935. The Unemployment Act covered all unemployed including the uninsured and for the first time tried to make a realistic assessment of household income. The first scales of payment to be introduced were too low, and provoked an angry and ultimately successful campaign to improve them which severely damaged the Conservative cause among the working class (although even in 1935 it attracted half their vote) for future generations. Baldwin, writing to the elder statesman Lord Salisbury, said it was the worst mess he had ever been associated with.

There was a recovery. It owed something to government economic policy. It owed much less to Baldwin than to Chamberlain, whose bent for administration and capacity for focus on a limited range of objectives made him a formidable operator in government. Baldwin's part was less heroic. He kept the national government together. An unsympathetic portrait was drawn, privately, by W P Crozier, editor of the *Manchester Guardian*, who met Baldwin for the first time in June 1934 and found his expectations of an amiable, possibly even whimsical individual quite mistaken. 'His face is rugged and nobbly ... [its] characteristic is determination and shrewdness – or rather, because it is much more than shrewdness, a sort of deep rustic craftiness ... in a rather grim and hard way. I got quite a new idea of him and for the first time understood how he had come to be leader of the Tory party and Prime Minister.'[8]

Baldwin had always had good personal relations with MacDonald. Now the two old men worked in a curious partnership, Baldwin increasingly covering for the ageing and ever weaker Prime Minister, protecting him from Tory assault and conspiracy and the problems caused by his deteriorating eyesight. By his involvement in specific areas of policy, particularly plans for India's future and on defence and disarmament matters, Baldwin rescued MacDonald from some of the consequences of his general inability to delegate. But Tom Jones thought his 'continued silence and passivity greatly weaken his influence and it is very difficult to bring him to the point of positive action'.[9] In June 1935, Geoffrey Dawson commented opaquely: 'How much of the cohesion of the National Government has been due to Mr Baldwin's temperament and character is a matter which history will assess and which perhaps only Mr MacDonald can yet appreciate fully.'[10]

Baldwin was 68 in 1935. He told his son Oliver that he began *to long for a lightening of the load*. Events were crowding in on him. The previous four years had been dominated more by wrestling with his party for the future of India than by concern for the economy. That was Chamberlain's domain. In 1935, the Government of India Act, passed into law. It was perhaps the greatest tangible achievement that MacDonald and Baldwin could claim. It was a starting point for independence, and although it was overtaken by events, it reconciled the subcontinent enough for it to be a source of strength rather than weakness in the Second World War. By 1935, however, focus had shifted back to Europe and the threat of war. Baldwin had become convinced of the need to rearm. Now he had to carry the public with him. He had one last educative mission to perform.

Chapter 7: Nerve and Sinew (1931–7)

If the Conservative party as a whole was tainted in the judgement of future generations by the hardness of its heart in the face of long-term mass unemployment, it was Baldwin's personal reputation that is still damaged by his lack of vigour in tackling rearmament. The debate over rearmament laid bare the weakness of a consensual approach to politics. Rearmament was difficult. Unlike Indian self-government, it was a question about which voters cared passionately. The arms race was blamed for the First World War. In a country that wanted peace and plenty, rearming promised only the threat of war and the transfer of spending from the home front to the defence industry. From 1930–7, spending on health and unemployment exceeded spending on defence for the only time in the 50-year period when a comparison can be made.[1] Until its final cancellation in 1934, Britain was still wrestling with the debt from the First World War.

The cause of peace was taken up across the country, across generations and across classes. In February 1933, Oxford undergraduates voted against fighting for king and country. In October of that year, the East Fulham by-election was lost to Labour after a campaign dominated by the question of rearmament (although subsequent analysis suggests people actually voted on more immediate concerns of bread and houses). In June 1935, the 'Peace Ballot' seemed to show that opinion remained opposed to preparing for war. There was more public sympathy for Germany, even after the rise of Hitler, who was expected to be another in Germany's progression of temporary leaders, than for France. For most of the 1930s, Labour, the main opposition party, was opposed to rearmament. Even after he was personally persuaded of the need to rearm, Baldwin hesitated to risk the trust of the country by demanding that they follow him where he believed they did not want to go. A Conservative election defeat at the hands of the socialists of the early 1930s would mean no rearmament at all. Ever since, Britain's foreign policy has been shaped by the belief that the national appetite for peace in those years was an invitation to the European dictators' appetite for aggression.

And there was Churchill. The most powerful exponent of rearmament was a man whose judgement Baldwin profoundly mistrusted. Winston Churchill had fought and lost to him over protection and resigned from the Shadow Cabinet[2] over India to try to 'shatter' the government from the backbenches, shamelessly exploiting his links with Baldwin's enemies, the newspaper barons. *He would sell his sword to anyone*, Baldwin told Rab Butler in 1935, and out of office, *felt himself completely at liberty to pursue what tactics he thought best.*[3] Churchill, Chancellor from 1925–9, had himself pared defence spending down from £119 million to £113 million. However, alerted by the ambitions of the

> **The Peace Ballot** was a survey with five questions conducted by the League of Nations Union. Eleven million people were questioned over a period of a year. It showed overwhelming support for arms limitation and non-military measures to back up League of Nations findings against aggressor nations. A majority, however, were prepared to accept that war might be justified as a last resort.

disarmament conference in Geneva in 1932 to allow France and Germany military parity, Churchill rapidly became a powerful critic of the government's position. Although they retained superficially easy personal relations, Baldwin elevated Churchill to a position alongside Lloyd George as the source of the government's problems. He would not bring him back into the shadow cabinet, and it seems unlikely that it was only because, as Baldwin famously indicated to a colleague, he wanted him to have clean hands should war finally be unavoidable. Churchill's taste for political combat was the antithesis of Baldwin's search for common ground. Ultimately, *The Gathering Storm*, Churchill's account of the years leading up to the outbreak of war that implied Baldwin had refused to campaign on rearmament because it would lose the election, was to make a notorious contribution to dragging down Baldwin's reputation.

Foreign and defence policy in the early 1930s was more than usually complex. Protecting the frontiers of an empire that embraced a quarter of the world's land mass required a large, modern navy; the escalating threat in Europe, and in particular Britain's underwriting of Europe's frontiers, a large modern army. Above all, Britain's domestic protection against the nightmare of the bomber demanded a large, modern air force to serve as both deterrent and defence. In 1928, perhaps the high water mark of aspirational foreign policy, Britain joined France, Italy and the United States (and ultimately more than 60 other countries) as signatories of the Kellogg-Briand pact which outlawed wars of aggression. In 1930, the Labour government, seeking arms control, negotiated the London Naval Treaty between the US, Japan and Britain that tightly restricted warship building.

Much sentimental ambition had been invested in the League of Nations as a peaceful way of guaranteeing international security, despite the absence from it of the United States and the later withdrawal of Germany, Japan and Italy. But as early as 1932 its inability to handle direct challenges was exposed by its tardy response to the Japanese invasion of Manchuria. Britain's instinctive preference for bilateral relations was demonstrated, after Japan moved on to Shanghai where there were direct British interests, in a readiness to overlook its old ally Japan's aggressive intentions. In 1932, the year the Geneva disarmament conference opened, staggered and then early in the following year, fell, Britain's service chiefs began to press for a reversal of the decline in defence spending. The 'Ten Year Rule', the assumption that Britain would not be involved in a major war in the next ten years, had governed military thinking since 1919. Now, despite the parlous economic circumstances, it was abandoned. Baldwin took over the chairmanship of the Committee on Imperial Defence (CID) from MacDonald, who was having persistent eye trouble and had to take leave of uncertain duration. Japanese aggression had not just exposed the weaknesses of the League, it had left Baldwin sceptical about economic sanctions, the principal non-military weapon at its disposal. Without America, and Russia, there could be no effective block on trade. And if economic sanctions were ineffective, they had to be backed up by a convincing threat of force.

I think it is well also for the man in the street to realise that there is no power on earth that can protect him from being bombed. Whatever people may tell him, the bomber will always get through.

BALDWIN

The CID agreed to reverse an earlier Labour decision and renew Singapore's defences, and expand those of Trincomalee, the main naval port in what was then Ceylon. On 9 November, Baldwin warned that Britain could not disarm unilaterally. The following day, the eve of Armistice Day, he made an extraordinary speech in the Commons in which he attempted to convey the catastrophic impact of modern warfare and the lack of strategic options. *I think it is well also for the man in the street to realise that there is no power on earth that can protect him from being bombed. Whatever people may tell him, the bomber will always get through. The only defence is in offence, which means that you have to kill more women and children more quickly than the enemy if you want to save yourselves.*[4]

As an exercise in warning of the realities of modern war, it achieved its desired effect. In a misunderstood peroration he challenged the country to demand that bombers should be banned (as, for example, the use of poison gas had been by the Third Geneva Protocol in 1925). To many, it sounded like defeatism; and there was a note of pessimism that can be attributed to the difficulties of a year in which the government had nearly fallen, he had faced powerful opposition over India, and he was carrying many of MacDonald's burdens. However, for some months to come, Baldwin appears genuinely to have sought a way of achieving aerial disarmament while at the same time supporting the rearmers in cabinet.

In January 1933, Hitler came to power; in March he assumed dictatorial powers; in October he pulled Germany out of the League of Nations. In November, a new cabinet sub-committee was established under the chairmanship of the Cabinet Secretary, Sir Maurice Hankey, and including the service chiefs and the permanent secretary to the Treasury, Sir Warren Fisher. It was to provide military and strategic advice, to prioritise the rearmament effort. Early in 1934, it reported that Britain was already trailing badly behind other world powers and was slipping further behind each year, that in both the Far East and Europe security was inadequate, but that defence requirements would mean the sacrifice of other programmes. Over five years, the committee recommended spending £72.2 million on upgrading the air force, and a further £13 million a year on naval construction, and even this, it warned, would barely improve Britain's defences enough to meet international obligations. But despite the involvement of Warren Fisher in drawing up the report, the Treasury declared that the proposed level of spending was unsustainable, and tried to reduce it by a third. Baldwin resisted but only succeeded in defending the navy. In March, Churchill challenged him: 'You must not go and ask the public what they think about [rearmament].' In the Commons a few days later, Baldwin trod a careful line between sounding militaristic and yet prepared, signalling that the assessment of threat was shifting from the Far East to Europe: *In air strength and in air power this country shall no longer be in a position inferior to any country within striking distance of our shore.* But he did not believe air parity would be enough. In July 1934 he warned, in words since levelled against him: *The greatest crime to our own people is to be afraid to tell the truth. The old frontiers are gone; when you think of the defence of England you no longer think of the chalk cliffs of Dover; you think of the Rhine. That is where our frontier lies.* The protection of the low countries, from where Germany could launch bombing raids on Britain, assumed strategic significance.

Hitler's behaviour grew more alarming. The Nazi leadership was bloodily purged. Concentration camps were opened up to incarcerate Communists and Jews. From Aix that summer, Baldwin wrote to Tom Jones that he thought the world had gone mad. In an interview with the editor of the *Manchester Guardian*, in which rearmament was only an afterthought in a long interview about India and Churchill, he admitted that *no one knows what the new Germany means*. In November, new evidence of German military preparations emerged. In a

Commons debate, Baldwin and Churchill again went head to head over the scale of rearmament. Churchill warned that by 1937, Germany's airforce would be nearly double Britain's. Baldwin accused him of exaggerating, but promised again that the RAF would always have at least parity. He did not, however, condemn Germany's rearmament despite its open breach of treaty obligations. The German press read this as acceptance. British foreign policy had been concentrated on trying to establish a balance of power in Europe against a French determination to stay ahead of its old aggressor and Germany's demand – sympathetically received in Britain – for military parity. It was felt that if Britain was aggressive towards Germany, France would redouble her own hostility.

Further alarming evidence of the scale of rearmament emerged. In March 1935, Hitler introduced compulsory military service. Days later he claimed to the Foreign Secretary Sir John Simon that his air force was already as strong as Britain's. In May, Baldwin told the Commons he had been wrong when he had claimed Britain was still 50 per cent ahead in air power; expanded production in Germany had allowed a much faster increase than he had anticipated. Diplomacy grew more frantic. Italy, France and Britain agreed the Stresa Front in April 1935, guaranteeing Austrian independence, promising to strengthen East European security and to preserve France's eastern frontiers. Soon afterwards France signed the Franco-Soviet non-aggression pact, inviting Bolshevik Russia to the west's high table in a way that some Conservatives found alarming; Baldwin was unhappy at the possibility of being required, in defence of France, to fight on the same side as the Bolsheviks. Britain signed a naval treaty with Germany that restricted the latter's navy to a third of Britain's. The Royal Navy was needed for the Far East, where Japan's military preparations appeared further advanced and more immediately threatening than Germany's. Baldwin (who had been involved in the negotiations for the naval treaty) saw it both as a successful example of arms limitation, and an early-warning device: any breach would be one more indication of Hitler's military intentions.

Late in 1934, domestic politics captured Baldwin's attention again. Ramsay MacDonald was ill, often confused and uncertain at the despatch box. Sir John Simon was considered disastrously indecisive as Foreign Secretary, and worse, given to blaming his officials for his own weakness. The Conservative Party was bored and fed up. Lloyd George had returned to the scene with a new programme that he unveiled in February 1935, an updated 'Yellow Book', challenging Baldwin to support him, making private overtures that some of the younger Tories wanted to pursue. Chamberlain refused to serve with him. The shambles over the unwittingly harsh new measures for unemployment assistance were provoking public disorder. Baldwin refused to move against MacDonald. It would precipitate an election and he was not confident of public opinion on the one issue that would dominate a campaign, rearmament. In May, the King celebrated his silver Jubilee amid moving scenes of popular rejoicing; on 5 June, the Government of India Act became law. On 7 June, MacDonald finally handed over the keys to Number 10. In its achievements, it had not been a happy partnership, although the lack of executive power had appealed to Baldwin's ruminative nature. Now, shortly before his 68th birthday, he became prime minister for the third time. An election would follow in the autumn. Hitler's militarism provoked a rush to defensive alliances and a spur to national rearmament that made a nonsense of the objectives of the League of Nations. It was a final irony that even as Europe prepared for war, the Peace Ballot recorded the League's great popularity among the 11.5m people it polled. Asked whether force would be justified against an aggressor, 6.8 million thought it would, but 4m or more thought it would not.

Baldwin reconstructed his Cabinet, replacing Simon at the Foreign Office with his old friend Samuel Hoare, and Anthony Eden, who had hoped for the promotion himself, moved into the Cabinet as League of Nations minister. Philip Cunliffe-Lister, shortly to inherit the title of Lord Swinton, became air minister. Churchill was not included. His behaviour over the India Act had made him unpopular in large parts of the party. And, as Baldwin wrote to Davidson, there was always the consideration that he *should be kept fresh to be our War Prime Minister.*[6] Instead, he was recruited to a sub-committee of the CID that was assessing air defence requirements, with his friend and adviser Professor Frederick Lindemann. In his first speech to the country as Prime Minister, Baldwin warned: *We are not satisfied with the defence of this country … We do not believe our defences are in that condition yet that will enable us to speak with the voice we should in favour of that collective security which is gradually commending itself to the people of this country.*

'There was much to be said for a League of Nations policy,' Harold Nicolson, a former diplomat, wrote with customary style in his biography of George V 'even as there was much to be said for a rapid return to the Balance of Power. But the two policies were mutually exclusive; to seek to combine them was to create disaster.'[5]

A further diplomatic crisis was now preoccupying the Foreign Office. In October 1934, Mussolini prepared to annex the larger part of Abyssinia. The French foreign minister, Pierre Laval, was unwilling to offend an important ally and indicated neutrality. Despite the abysmal nature of what would now be called the human rights record of its ruler, Haile Selassie, Abyssinia was a member of the League of Nations and Britain insisted on the use of its reconciliation procedures. Italy asserted that Africa was beyond them. Like France, Britain too was anxious not to offend Italy, for fear of encouraging a pact between the Axis powers. Preserving Italy as an ally was part of the increasingly desperate attempt to keep Germany isolated and to preserve the independence of Austria. All through 1935 the crisis ran on, interwoven with other alarming developments. It had emerged that Germany was borrowing £1,000 million a year to finance rearmament and could be ready for war in January 1939. Baldwin began to talk of abandoning financial constraints to go flat out on defence. Attempts to find a (less than honourable) way of reconciling Italy to the League of Nations intervention failed, but Baldwin was unwilling to take the risk of finding Britain alone in trying to ensure that League sanctions were observed, a fear magnified by the determination of France to sustain its friendship with Italy rather than prop up the League. British warships were sent to the Mediterranean, but France made it clear they would be allowed no access to her own southern ports. On 3 October, Italy invaded Abyssinia, having first, in a grim precedent of a savage campaign that included the use of poison gas, bombed a hospital storehouse flying the Red Cross. In London, Baldwin took advantage of this renewed evidence of European instability to push through a £200 million naval programme and to instigate plans to accelerate rearmament programmes for both the army and air force.

Soon afterwards, ignoring Labour's charge of cynically exploiting national fears of war, Baldwin called an election. Rearmament was portrayed as a necessary precondition of peace. He produced another memorable address, 'Bound over to make the peace', to the Peace Society on 31 October. He was no warmonger, he said, as once again he conjured up distant images of English rural life and, in one of his brilliant phrases, the little things that mark the *boundary stones of our spiritual estate. To what risks do we expose our treasures – irreplaceable treasures, for you cannot build up beauty like that in a few years of mass-production. Make no mistake; every piece of all the life that we and our fathers have made in this land, every thing we have and hold and cherish, is in jeopardy in this great issue* [of rearming]. Britain, he said, must make the peace; but it could not be done without access to force to back up persuasion. *Weakness, or wavering, or uncertainty, or neglect of our obligations – obligations for peace – doubts of our own safety, give no assurance of peace... . But we have gone too far alone, and must try to bring others along with us. I give you my word that there will be no great armaments.*

The speech received wide acclaim. Rearmament, often mentioned expressly as a way of underwriting collective security, was not the only issue in the election – unemployment still stood at two million – but the result was generally interpreted as a mandate to rearm. Labour, campaigning on a generally pacifist platform showed only a very partial recovery, winning 154 seats to the Conservatives' 432, with 53 per cent of the vote. Baldwin, Tom Jones thought, had played his hand faultlessly. The discontents of the past year were largely forgotten. But his lack of interest in detail and the relaxed confidence with which he habitually regarded his ministers almost immediately betrayed him into one of the worst misjudgements of his political career.

The Abyssinian crisis intensified and further exposed the

weakness of both Britain and the League. Britain could not risk engaging in a war against Italy alone, but France did not want to fight Italy and there was no other ally. On 2 December, Hoare set off for France on holiday, following a period of strain that had prompted fainting fits for which his doctor prescribed a period of complete rest. Nonetheless, he proposed to stop over in Paris to meet Laval to explore again ways of achieving a peaceful settlement. He had no specific instructions from Cabinet except to bring back any proposals for approval. Over a period of two days, Hoare and Laval, aided by Robert Vansittart, the Permanent Under-Secretary at the Foreign Office, drew up a scheme to dismember Abyssinia. Hoare then went on to his skating holiday. Vansittart disappeared. The 'formula', which had to be put not only to the British cabinet but to Italy, Abyssinia and the League of Nations, was leaked to the French press. Public opinion was outraged, not only by the terms but by the attempt to circumvent the League, which Hoare in September had boldly praised in terms that encouraged people at home and abroad to see it as the sheet anchor of Britain's foreign policy. This view was encouraged by the tone of the general election campaign. Baldwin went to the Commons and in an untypically clumsy expression that indicated his confusion, he declared that if only he could tell them all that he knew no one would go into the lobby against him, a situation he summed up in a single disastrous phrase, *my lips are not yet unsealed*.[7] Privately, he believed Laval was in Mussolini's pay and there was no question of them fighting over Abyssinia. For months afterwards the cartoonist David Low depicted Baldwin with sticking plaster across his mouth. *The stupidest thing I ever said,* he acknowledged later.

The Cabinet rebelled. At least half declared that unless Hoare resigned, they would. Baldwin had to choose between

Hoare-Laval Pact

'There is an awkward sequel to Mr. Baldwin's triumph, for the sake of which we may sacrifice chronology. His Foreign Secretary, Sir Samuel Hoare, travelling through Paris to Switzerland on a well-earned skating holiday, had a talk with M. Laval, still French Foreign Minister. The result of this was the Hoare-Laval pact of December 9. It is worth while to look a little into the background of this celebrated incident. The idea of Britain leading the League of Nations against Mussolini's Fascist invasion of Abyssinia had carried the nation in one of its big swings. But once the election was over and the Ministers found themselves in possession of a majority which might give them for five years the guidance of the State, many tiresome consequences had to be considered. At the root of them all lay Mr. Baldwin's "There must be no war", and also "There must be no large rearmaments". This remarkable Party Manager, having won the election on world leadership against aggression, was profoundly convinced that we must keep peace at any price ... The new House of Commons was a spirited body. With all that lay before them in the next ten years, they had need to be. It was therefore with a horrible shock that, while tingling from the election, they received the news that a compromise had been made between Sir Samuel Hoare and M. Laval on Abyssinia. This crisis nearly cost Mr. Baldwin his political life ... Mr. Baldwin fell almost overnight from his pinnacle of acclaimed national leadership to a depth where he was derided and despised. His position in the House during these days was pitiful. He had never understood why people should worry about all these bothersome foreign affairs. They had a Conservative majority and no war. What more could they want? But the experienced pilot felt and measured the full force of the storm.

The Cabinet, on December 9, had approved the Hoare-Laval plan to partition Abyssinia between Italy and the Emperor. On the 13th the full text of the Hoare-Laval proposals was laid before the League. On the 18th the Cabinet abandoned the Hoare-Laval proposals, thus entailing the resignation of Sir Samuel Hoare. [Churchill, Winston: *The Second World War*, Volume 1, The Gathering Storm. Cassell & Co., 1948, p.141–4] his friend and his government. Hoare, farcically, had had another blackout while skating and broken his nose. He could not immediately travel home. Forced to resign, he spoke from the backbenches on 19 December, in justification of his reversion to *realpolitik*. The League, he suggested, had neither the will nor the means to force Italy to back down. Mussolini was 'getting more than he had, though less than he would take', Vansittart, the real architect of the deal, observed. Others disagreed. In the boldest act of its existence, the League had agreed to apply sanctions. They had been given no chance to take effect. It should be added that Mussolini had warned that an attempt to starve Italy of oil would be treated as a *casus belli*. He would have had little trouble obtaining oil from the US, where the administration lacked the power to prevent trade with a foreign country. Nonetheless, British voters, for so long Baldwin's great concern, felt duped. In May, Mussolini annexed the whole of Abyssinia in what for the time was a uniquely bloody and one-sided conquest. The emperor Haile Selassie was forced into exile in England. Baldwin made a humble apology in the Commons for underestimating the national conscience. Eden was appointed to the Foreign Office, but only after Baldwin had offended Austen Chamberlain, who had been led to believe he was to be recalled to arms, and in graceless terms appointed the 38-year-old Eden. *It looks as if it will have to be you.*[8]

Rearmament began in earnest. In February, Baldwin announced an increase of £394 million over five years. He stopped short of appointing a Minister for Defence to oversee the often-difficult relations between the services, and to make strategic decisions about priorities in rearmament, but instead created the job of Minister for Defence Co-ordination. He resisted pressure to give the job to Churchill, not least because its holder would have to deputise for him in a way that might have encouraged Churchill to be viewed as his successor. Instead – perhaps with a deliberate lack of tact – he appointed the Attorney General, Sir Thomas Inskip, who had fallen out with Churchill in a recent incident involving parliamentary privilege. Baldwin's first hope had been to make amends for the fiasco of the Hoare-Laval pact by reinstalling Hoare, a second-rank politician of ambition so naked that only Baldwin himself appeared unaware of his determination to become Prime Minister as soon as possible. Instead, to general disapproval, Hoare returned as First Lord of the Admiralty. Later he became Home Secretary.

In March 1936, in a long-anticipated move, Hitler marched into the Rhineland. It was an open breach of the Locarno Treaty to which, unlike Versailles, Germany had been a willing signatory. The British public thought it was Hitler's backyard, and had no desire to go to war over it, particularly since Hitler offered to rejoin the League and made apparently generous offers of bilateral non-aggression pacts. When France's new Foreign Secretary, Flandin, demanded sanctions, Baldwin told him it was impossible. They could not work without military back up, and Britain was not prepared for war. He told cabinet that war would bring Russia in and it would end in Germany going Communist. Hitler's generals had warned him against the military re-occupation. They had orders to stop if challenged. By 1939, it seemed clear that the countdown to war had begun at this moment three years earlier.

In May, Baldwin told Eden that he wanted to get closer to Hitler ('How?' asked Eden. 'I have no idea,' replied Baldwin, 'that is your job.'[9]); he hoped that the next war Germany would fight would be against the Soviet Union, where Stalin had embarked on the first show trials and purges. This line of thought was indicated both to individual backbenchers and then in July to a group led by Churchill that came for a briefing on the state of the rearmament programme. *I do not believe [Germany] wants to move West because West would be a difficult programme for her, and if she does it before we are ready I quite agree the picture is perfectly awful,* he told Churchill. *If there is any fighting in Europe to be done, I should like to see the Bolshies and the Nazis doing it.*[10] Churchill had already warned a Commons committee that if Britain let Germany expand eastwards, 'Within a year Germany would become dominant from Hamburg to the Black Sea, and we should

If there is any fighting in Europe to be done, I should like to see the Bolshies and the Nazis doing it.

BALDWIN

be faced by a confederacy such as had never been seen since Napoleon.'[11] There is no evidence that Baldwin's thoughts were other than an aspiration. In his first note to British Embassies from the Foreign Office, Eden warned that the German Chancellor, set on European dominance and the capture of raw materials, could expand in either direction. He added that German policy was to divide the English from the French.

In Spain, General Franco's Nationalist forces attacked the left-wing Popular Front government. Britain and France adopted a policy of non-intervention. The dictators adopted it as a surrogate for a wider war, Soviet communists fighting alongside the left, the fascists fighting with German and Italian armaments. The future of Europe seemed starkly divided between fascist and communist, and the Conservatives were more frightened of the latter than the former.

Baldwin was exhausted and demoralised. Some of his colleagues wondered if he was on the brink of a complete breakdown. On doctor's orders, he took a long holiday, but for the first time since 1922 he stayed in England, in 'constant touch' with his Foreign Secretary. Eden reported later that 'constant touch' involved a letter and a phone call, both of which related to a forthcoming weekend visit. In November, in the autumn debate on defence in the Commons, he made another infelicitous remark. When he had met Churchill in July, he had justified the considerations that stopped him coming out more openly for rearmament. The first thing to do in a democracy, he explained, was to get a mandate. As soon as he felt the country was ready, he called an election and in 1935 the need for rearmament had been accepted. For Baldwin, this was almost a truism, and he perhaps failed to understand how it could be misunderstood. When he repeated it, in the Commons, it was wilfully misconstrued by Churchill, and it dogs his reputation still. Replying to a brilliant Churchill attack ('The Government cannot make up their minds, or they cannot get the Prime Minister to make up his mind. So they go on, in strange paradox, decided only be undecided, resolved to be irresolute, adamant for drift, solid for fluidity, all-powerful to be impotent'), Baldwin justified the slow start to rearmament by referring to the need to persuade the public of the need. He was talking specifically about public opinion as expressed in the East Fulham by-election of 1933. The way he phrased the sentiment, however, left many listeners with the impression that he had been talking not about that by-election, but the much more recent general election. To a politician like Churchill with a predator's eye for vulnerability, it was the moment when Baldwin admitted to putting party before country. Although others claimed that there was a sharp intake of breath, a close observer like Harold Nicolson noticed a quite different effect. '[Baldwin] speaks slowly with evident physical effort. At one moment he loses his notes. It is all very well done but he has a poor case... . by the end of his speech, his voice and thought limp as if he were a tired walker on a long road. The House realises that the dear old man has come to the end of his vitality.'[12]

If Baldwin's ambition had been to bring the country to face the need for rearmament, in the end he had succeeded. But he was not pursuing the cause, nor was he conducting a foreign policy likely to convince Hitler that he was to be resisted rather than conciliated. It was time to hand power to a younger, more energetic man. But his resolve to retire was abandoned in the face of another constitutional crisis.

Chapter 8: Or walk with Kings: The Abdication Crisis 1936

Baldwin's last full year as Prime Minister began with a curious personal triumph. On 19 January 1936, the King's doctor, Lord Dawson, announced that 'the King's life was drawing peacefully to a close'. Less than 24 hours later, he was dead. Baldwin was already shattered by the death the night before of his beloved cousin Rudyard Kipling. George V's death was a blow of a different order, but they had worked in a relationship of mutual respect for 15 years. Each embodied virtues the other valued highly: a sense of duty and public service, a straightforwardness in the conduct of business, a desire for consensus. Baldwin's conduct at the time of the formation of the national government had particularly impressed the Palace. 'The King was greatly pleased with Mr Baldwin's readiness to meet the crisis which had arisen, and to sink Party interests for the sake of the Country',[2] his secretary Sir Clive Wigram noted. The friendship was never personal, like the intimacy the King shared with the railwaymen's leader Jimmy Thomas, who used to spend a fortnight at Balmoral every year, but each had a high opinion of the other's judgement and opinions.

Baldwin's ability to express the mood of the nation, to

If in any cataclysm the Crown vanished, the Empire would vanish with it.[1]

BALDWIN

make people feel they were made of nobler stuff than they had realised, perhaps never met a greater triumph than in his broadcast on the death of the King. In his slightly dated style, he spoke of the duties of kingship that were now the new King's legacy: *He inherits an example of kingly conduct, of virtue, of wisdom, of endurance... .*[George] *earned the loyalty and respect of all parties in the State, new and old. He hands down in turn to his son the throne he himself received from his father, and he hands it down with its foundations strengthened, its moral authority, its honour and its dignity enhanced.*[3] A million people filed past the coffin where the old King lay in state. Millions more lined the route as his coffin was taken from Westminster Abbey to Windsor.

Baldwin gave monarchy a meaning that might otherwise have been lost in the birth of mass democracy. In the British constitution, he told audiences, the monarchy was the bulwark against the kind of tyranny that threatened Europe. It was a keystone of the state, *as native to our country and to our people as oak or ash or thorn*, he said. The monarch represented the continuity and evolution of the constitution, but he was also a reflection of contemporary Britain, an expression of national character and public values, imbued with what Baldwin called *great moral power*. This was a description of George V's monarchy, one that the King himself would have recognised. But the institution did not itself create the qualities that its holder needed. Baldwin had heard George express his doubts about his son's capacity for kingship. 'After I am dead the boy will ruin himself within twelve months.' Within weeks of his father's death, the conduct of Edward VIII was causing alarm.

Edward was 41 when his father died, handsome, charming, popular, unmarried and becoming a potential political liability. He was sympathetic to Germany and openly admired the Nazis; after leaks of sensitive material were traced to the Palace, MI6 put him under close scrutiny. He had had a series of affairs with married women. When the Prince of Wales first encountered Wallis Simpson, he was awaiting the return of his current girlfriend, Lady Furness, from the United States. Mrs Simpson was twice married, once divorced, and an American. After George's death, eyebrows were raised when she and her husband began to appear in the Court Circular, the daily diary of royal activity. But the presence of Mr Simpson satisfied the proprieties. In the summer of 1936, to the great excitement of the foreign press, she was among a small party which, with the new King, cruised round the Mediterranean in a chartered yacht. The British press reported nothing, but in America and in Europe it was a front-page story. In October, Baldwin returned from the prolonged break he had taken on doctor's orders and began to catch up with his correspondence. What he called the *King's matter* immediately caught his attention. It was not only cuttings from the foreign press, but complaints about the King's conduct from courtiers (whose numbers had been reduced and whose pay had been cut). They reported that official engagements were dropped and important papers lay unread so that his pursuit of Mrs Simpson might continue. A popular but idle King was a problem: a popular but idle King set on marriage to a divorced foreigner was a constitutional crisis.

On 14 October, Baldwin had an inconclusive meeting with Edward, whom he knew well from their travels together in 1927, when the Baldwins had accompanied the then Prince of Wales to Canada. Baldwin liked Edward and it was an awkward encounter. On 15 October, Sir Alex Hardinge, the King's secretary, discovered that Mrs Simpson was suing her husband for divorce, in Ipswich. On 16 October, the King invited the press barons Beaverbrook and Rothermere to

Balmoral and flattered them into agreeing that they would print nothing for the time being.

If Baldwin had hoped to be able to follow his customary ruminative approach to problem solving, a weekend in the company of the Roman Catholic Viceroy of Ireland, his uncle the Duke of Norfolk (who as Earl Marshal was to organise the Coronation), and the press baron Lord Kelmsley, punctuated by visits from Hardinge pressing him to intervene, made it impossible for him to sit back. On the following Tuesday, 20 October he met the King at his retreat in Windsor, Fort Belvedere. Baldwin had a whisky and soda and told him the people did not like his association with Mrs Simpson. He suggested the King intervene to stop the divorce. Otherwise, he warned, the press would abandon their restraint. Public opinion would be outraged. The Dominions would be perturbed. The King declared that Mrs Simpson was 'the only woman in the world and I cannot live without her'. Even so, Baldwin shied away from the question of marriage, suggesting only that Mrs Simpson go abroad for a prolonged period. He departed with a pleasant suggestion for replanting the herbaceous border.

On 27 October, Mrs Simpson was granted a decree nisi. In a matter of months, she would be free to remarry. The British press stayed silent. Baldwin was desperate to avoid the open confrontation between King and government that he felt would erupt the moment the news became general, inviting the country to take sides between King and Parliament. Baldwin had no doubt that Mrs Simpson would be unacceptable as Queen to Britain or the Dominions. That summer, a senior trade unionist had allowed his mistress to act as hostess at TUC functions, and found none of the wives would shake her hand. As Lord Kelmsley had warned Baldwin, the Nonconformist conscience was not dead. Harold Nicolson observed later in the scandal, 'The upper classes mind her being an American more than they mind her being divorced. The lower classes do not mind her being an American but loathe the idea that she has had two husbands already.'[4] (Some of the aristocracy still detested divorce. The second Viscount Halifax – father of Lord Irwin – believed murder to be better than divorce, 'as it did less damage to the moral side of the family unit.'[5]) Yet the Hearst newspapers in America were already announcing the impending marriage.

The more activist members of the Cabinet wanted to do something immediately. Led by Chamberlain, they prepared an edict that they wanted Baldwin to present to the King, demanding that he end his 'association' with Mrs Simpson 'forthwith'. Otherwise the government would resign. For the time being, the document remained private. Meanwhile the Governor General of Canada, Lord Tweedsmuir, wrote to warn that the American reports were now reluctantly believed and the results would be damaging and possibly disastrous for this vital yet fragile part of the Empire. Hardinge, aware that the press could not be held much longer, and also that it was possible the divorce proceedings might be scuppered by an allegation of collusion that required the intervention of the King's Proctor (an officer of the Crown who would investigate allegations of irregularity, in this case possibly by the King himself) wrote to set the facts before the King. These included the possibility that the government might resign if he persisted in his attentions to Mrs Simpson. It seemed highly unlikely that there would be a majority in the Commons in favour of a marriage and

'The upper classes mind her {Wallis Simpson} being an American more than they mind her being divorced. The lower classes do not mind her being an American but loathe the idea that she has had two husbands already.'

HAROLD NICOLSON

therefore willing to form a new government. The alternative was an election that would make it the subject, in effect, of a referendum. Mrs Simpson must retreat beyond the reach of the British press, at once.

Baldwin, meanwhile, had been shown Chamberlain's ultimatum threatening resignation. Baldwin was appalled. Typically, however, he merely asked for time to think. Nothing more was heard of the challenge, but it emerged soon afterwards in a different form. At this point, the Australian High Commissioner in London, Stanley Bruce, arrived on the scene to sharpen the Prime Minister's focus. After a lunch at which he gleaned the essential facts of the case, he sent an *aide-mémoire* that concluded with advice on how to avert the ultimate crisis, of the King trying to appeal over the heads of his government. Baldwin must tell him that marriage was unacceptable in Britain and the Dominions; that the King himself would suffer; Parliament would take action through the Civil List and there would be a demand for his abdication. If he refused to abdicate, or to abandon Mrs Simpson, then Baldwin must tell him he and his government would resign.

On 9 November, a second letter arrived from Lord Tweedsmuir in Canada warning that the American press 'tattle' was being taken very seriously. There was enough in the letter for some to believe that there was a risk that Canada might secede. On 16 November, a further meeting between Baldwin and the King took place. It was a curious reverse of the process by which Baldwin had first become prime minister, when George V had recognised that in the public mind Baldwin was more acceptable than Lord Curzon. Now it was Baldwin pressing George's son to realise that he could not choose as his Queen a woman whom the great majority of the British people, and the people of the Dominions, would reject. The

King's response was uncompromising. 'I have looked at it from all sides – and I mean to marry Mrs Simpson.' He would abdicate. That night he saw his mother, Queen Mary, and his brother, the Duke of York. They could not change his mind.

The following day, the King toured the South Wales coalfields to an enthusiastic reception. Rothermere's *Daily Mail* billed the King's South Wales visit as a pleasing contrast to the lack of interest in the plight of the unemployed shown by the government. The King's friends – led by Rothermere's son Esmond and with Churchill somewhere in the background, suspected of offering to form a government – approached him with the idea that rather than abdicate he make a morganatic marriage with Mrs Simpson, so that she could be his wife without sharing his royal privileges and duties. On 19 November, Baldwin was reassured by Walter Monckton, the King's legal adviser, and Hardinge, that the decision to abdicate would not be reversed. But when Baldwin met the King on 25 November to discuss it, Edward, buoyed by his reception in South Wales and convinced he had popular support, now pressed the argument for a morganatic marriage. Baldwin, hoping to give him the opportunity to understand the gravity of the proposal, said that in that case he must put it to the Cabinet and to the Dominion prime ministers. It was a formal procedure, and the King would in effect be bound by its findings. Beaverbrook, without success, tried to persuade the King to delay. He was immovable. On 27 November, the Cabinet was fully briefed for the first time, and made aware of the formidable danger of the King and government in confrontation, the government resigning, to be replaced by a Churchill-led King's party. On 28 November, Churchill, in the rearmament debate, delivered his damning 'decided to be undecided speech' and Baldwin was observed looking rattled and tired. On 29 November, Beaverbrook who had been working to build support for the King, was warned that the cabinet was united in its opposition to the King's marriage. The replies from the Dominions began to come in: they were universally hostile to the idea of a morganatic marriage, and accepted that abdication was the least bad solution. The King was already thought too damaged to be able to restore authority to the monarchy.

On 2 December, the *Yorkshire Post*, reporting an address by the Bishop of Bradford, opened the floodgates for the press. That night, Baldwin saw the King again in a tense and difficult encounter. Cabinet, he said, would not accept a morganatic marriage. The King countered with his conviction that the people would support him. *To all arguments based on responsibility towards his people,* Baldwin complained to his wife later, *the King did not react, not feeling any responsibility which should dictate or influence his conduct.*[6] On 3 December, Mrs Simpson was finally persuaded to flee to France for her own protection. That evening Baldwin and the King met again. Edward proposed that he should put his dilemma to the people, and showed him the text of a broadcast he wanted to make to set out his case. This was the move Baldwin most feared. He warned the King of the dangers,

To all arguments based on responsibility towards his people the King did not react, not feeling any responsibility which should dictate or influence his conduct.

BALDWIN

both personal and constitutional. That afternoon, Churchill had spoken at a great rearmament rally in the Albert Hall without directly mentioning the King, but the papers the following morning, 4 December, contained oblique indications of Churchill's support for him and Mrs Simpson. Later that day, the Cabinet declared it unconstitutional for the King to speak without the advice of his ministers. The Cabinet wanted a swift resolution, and pushed Baldwin again to issue an ultimatum. Baldwin resisted, but at a further meeting with the King told him that a broadcast was out of the question, and stressed – without putting a timescale on it – the need for a quick resolution. That evening, Churchill dined with the King and appealed to him to stay. The following day he sent an account of the conversation to Baldwin warning of the King's extreme distress – 'he appeared to me driven to the last extremity of endurance'. But the King was now aware of the unattractive crowd of followers he was attracting, notably Mosely's fascist Blackshirts. The King was again ready to abdicate. On the evening of 5 December, Baldwin went again to Fort Belvedere where the King begged him to legislate to grant Mrs Simpson her decree absolute at once. In return, he would quietly abdicate and leave the country. The King later thought there was a deal. Baldwin warned that it was a contentious proposal that he was unlikely to be able to meet. It seems Cabinet would not accept it. The plea now became to allow the King a little more time. Cabinet would not even let him wait until Christmas. He was to be given until Tuesday. On Monday 7 December, MPs returned from their constituencies after a break from the seething excitement of Westminster, having learnt that there was no support in the country for a King's party. As Baldwin made another holding statement, an attempt by Churchill to intervene was howled down. Churchill had already been warned by Beaverbrook, 'our cock won't fight'. The following day, Baldwin packed an overnight bag and took himself to Belvedere to sit with the King while he reached his final decision. Faced with the prospect of being closeted overnight with his Prime Minister, Edward declared he could not be moved from his decision to abdicate. They dined, with the King's brothers. According to a popular tale of the time, the Prime Minister and the King shed tears.

On Wednesday, Mrs Simpson made it clear she would stop her divorce and renounce the King. But Edward was now fixed on abdication. On the morning of 10 December, he signed the Instrument of Abdication. In his diary that night, Harold Nicolson described the scene in the Commons: 'The [Speaker] rises and reads out the message of Abdication in a quavering voice. The feeling that at any moment he may break down from emotion increases our own emotion. I have never known in any assemblage such accumulation of pity and terror.' Then Baldwin gave the first full account of the events of the past month. Nicolson called it 'tragic in its simplicity'. Baldwin's notes had become muddled, and he occasionally lost the date of the specific event he was describing and turned to Hoare, sitting beside him, for help. 'The artifice of such asides is so effective that one imagines it to be deliberate. There is no moment when he overstates emotion or indulges in oratory. There is intense silence broken only by the reporters in the gallery scuttling away to telephone the speech paragraph by paragraph ... When it was over [Attlee, leader of the Opposition] asked that the sitting might be adjourned till 6 p.m. We file out broken in body and soul, conscious that we have heard the best speech that we shall ever hear in our lives. There was no question of applause. It was the silence of Gettysburg.'[7]

Baldwin emerged more popular than he had been since the triumphant and peaceful resolution of the General Strike ten years earlier. On both occasions there was a sense that he had led the nation through a time of great peril with calm judgement and a fine ear for popular sentiment. At Sandringham in January he and the new King, George VI, shared the cheers of a crowd of 8,000. He was on the home run now. It was fixed that he would retire at Whitsun, after the Coronation which was to be on 12 May. There was no question but that his successor would be Chamberlain. Bruised by successive reverses over India and the Abdication and the pace of rearmament, uncharacteristically pessimistic about his ability to influence debate, Churchill had temporarily retreated from the politics of the front line to complete the final volume of his biography of the first Duke of Marlborough.

Of all the anticipated consequences of the Abdication Crisis, the one that mattered most was the least expected. The future arrangements of the Duke of Windsor, as Edward became, provoked some unpleasant rows about money. But otherwise the former King behaved well, and the new King showed himself to be his father's son. There was a period of relative quiet on the political front. As a result, the government's eyes turned inward, away from foreign affairs, to worthwhile projects like the raising of the school leaving age to 15. The temporary extinction of the Churchillian power of creating debate and shaping the public mind was badly needed. The previous October, the Rome-Berlin Axis was created. But in the spring, Chamberlain insisted on slowing defence spending again by extending the completion date for the latest air programme and woefully under-equipping the army. (At the same time the German finance minister was also arguing that the economy could not sustain Hitler's rearmament programme, but Hitler overruled him.) Turning parts of industry over to military production, as the European powers were doing, was still considered unduly militaristic. Hopes remained pinned to making a deal with Germany, perhaps creating a successor to the Locarno Treaty, so casually broken when Hitler reoccupied the Rhineland. Talking loudly about rearmament was considered bad diplomacy. A Cabinet sub-committee had asked the BBC not to carry dissenting voices on the European issue. In Spain, where the dictators' interference in the Civil War was unmistakable and bloody

— the planes that bombed Guernica were German, escorted by Italian Fiat fighters — Eden's efforts to get Britain to back France in making a reality of non-intervention were disregarded. Baldwin's last five months in office were marred by his tacit acceptance of a decision to abandon military parity in favour of a level of armaments capable only of deterrence. It was to have a profound impact on the diplomatic options open in the final years before the outbreak of war.

On 12 May 1937, the new King and Queen were crowned in Westminster Abbey. Baldwin was again loudly cheered. Fulsome tributes followed a little more than a fortnight later, when he spoke in the Commons for the final time. He became a Knight of the Garter, and soon the first Earl Baldwin of Bewdley.

Until 1940, he had a statesman's retirement. He and Lucy lived mainly back at Astley, ten miles or so from the place of his birth, but they spent some time in London each year. He was Chancellor of Cambridge University until his death, and visited frequently. He gave dinner parties for George VI to introduce him to the Labour leaders. He saw his political friends. After Eden's resignation over the direction of foreign policy in early 1938, they discussed tactics. There was even speculation that Baldwin might return to active politics. After Munich, he praised Chamberlain for buying more time while disagreeing

> **Baldwin's old friend Geoffrey Dawson** wrote in the *Times*, 'More than any of the predecessors to whom the title has been applied, he has been a "House of Commons man" ... He believed profoundly in the democratic system, and the House of Commons was its mainspring and focus... . The crowds who gave him so signal a reception as he passed in the Coronation pageant ... cheered him just because they had come to look upon him as the embodiment of their own best instincts.'[8]

with his decision to embark on personal diplomacy. Not until Dunkirk in 1940 was the happily-occupied retirement of a distinguished statesman interrupted. Over a weekend Michael Foot and two colleagues, all employees of Lord Beaverbrook's on the *Evening Standard*, wrote *The Guilty Men*, under the pseudonym Cato, indicting Baldwin and Chamberlain and their governments for negligence and hinting in some cases at fascist sympathies. (Later one of the three contributors joined Moral Rearmament and visited Astley to apologise for the untruths he had written.) With Chamberlain dead, Baldwin became the villain; he was persecuted with hate mail and publicly reviled. Humiliatingly, the dozen or so iron gates around the Astley gardens which had originally been granted exemption on artistic grounds from the programme to turn metal into war materiel, were ordered to be taken down. Lord Reith, the former Director-General of the BBC, was now in government and was the final arbiter. He made no move to intervene. Only the main gates, given by his constituency on his retirement in 1937, were to be spared – to protect him from the mob, a Conservative backbencher jeered.

In the summer of 1945, Lucy died. Baldwin himself clung on, forlorn and lonely, being interviewed by G M Young, his official biographer, for what became an ungenerous and unsatisfactory account of his life, until a few months after his 80th birthday. He died in his sleep during the night of 13 December. An appeal for a fund for a memorial raised a paltry amount. But Churchill, who was to poison his memory, was a generous donor, and came to speak at its unveiling. 'He was the most formidable politician I have ever known in public life.'

Part Three

THE LEGACY

Chapter 9: The Baldwin Era

The heart of the country is sound, but it wants watching.
(1) It is a remarkable thing that ever since the war we have
had a Right Government, although, with the extension of
the Franchise and the influx of subversive ideas, one would
have expected otherwise. (2) As soon as the 1926 strike was
over, employers and employed settled down to work without
resentment. (3) No less remarkable was the way in which the
Labour Opposition worked the Parliamentary machine from
1931–1935, only a handful of them, instead of sulking as
they might well have done.[1]

In November, six months after he had retired, a valedictory
dinner was organised for Baldwin at the Athenaeum. His
speech, which lasted for more than half an hour, was a political
testament, a memoir that imposed a pattern on a life that
even friends had sometimes thought little more than a series
of crises from which he was rescued only by his unique ability
to inspire trust. Baldwin's theme was stability and unity. He
had come to power as the nation adapted to universal suffrage
and the power of organised labour. He touched on his efforts
to embrace the Labour party as a legitimate party of power,
the cathartic effect of the General Strike, and the moment of
victory in 1931 when unemployed men and women voted
in favour of a cut in unemployment benefit because they

understood it was necessary for the good of the country. Although it was a party gathering, he spoke of neither the Conservatives nor Conservatism, nor defence nor foreign affairs, but devoted more than half the speech to the excellent leadership the opposition had enjoyed – the pacifist George Lansbury as much as the self-sacrificing Ramsay MacDonald. The Baldwin monument, he suggested, would be found in the health of democracy in the late 1930s.

Most prime ministers, in the end, are remembered unkindly. But few can have retired amid such glory and lived to endure such vilification, accused of wilful incompetence and selfish indifference. Churchill's memoirs only confirmed the indictment of Baldwin for failing to anticipate the threat from the dictators. Labour successfully attributed to him the responsibility for allowing the working class to suffer through the long years of depression. Both these interpretations were political in their inspiration. Although they are not without some basis in fact they are both partisan readings of Baldwin's career, made for political purposes. Curiously, even the charges demonstrate a greater success. Britain came through economic catastrophe without revolution, survived the disasters of Dunkirk and the Blitz without civil unrest and won the war despite the military shortcomings – before, with Labour's first landslide in 1945, undergoing an extraordinary transfer of power which was accepted without resort to undemocratic resistance. Class war, that nightmare of the 1920s, became the dog that did not bark. As Baldwin had once told the Junior Imperial League they must, he had made democracy safe for the world.

Baldwin's valedictory at the Athenaeum was not only a politician's rationalisation after the event. Nor was his understanding of the task he faced when he first became prime minister unique. At the time when Baldwin was still uncommitted to a political career, the Conservative historian Keith Feiling had warned: 'The old Toryism is dead ... The old Toryism is one of the outworn beliefs that hang on to cumber a newborn earth. What place shall we find for it in an age of unrest, scepticism, speed, experiment?'[2] Neville Chamberlain (of whom Feiling later wrote the official biography) had told his sister 'unless we leave our mark as social reformers, the country will take it out of us hereafter'. Until 1922, the Conservatives had not won an election on their own account since the turn of the century. Without the afterglow of victory in a World War that had carried them to power as part of a coalition in 1918, there was no clear idea of where it could find a new parliamentary majority. There was no certainty that the party would survive. Lloyd George was known to want to attract its stars for a new centre party, dedicated to the cause around which the right could unite: crushing socialism.

Baldwin was temperamentally opposed to the undemocratic implications of such a project. The danger of conflict, the purposes of democracy, and the body of classical thought from which his ideas derived were the subjects of many of his most effective speeches. Their power in turn was reinforced by his conduct in political life, from the destruction of the corruptly pragmatic Lloyd George coalition through his generosity to his opponents, his studied respect for the electoral mandate (on protection as well as rearmament, although his reputation was damaged by the Hoare-Laval Pact) and the distance he tried to keep between himself and Tory ideologues. Baldwin's hero was Disraeli, but not the flashy, clever sweet-talking Disraeli. His Disraeli was the Disraeli of one nation and the search for national unity. Baldwin's instinct was always for peace through conciliation and accommodation. A childhood story describes him becoming increasingly silent as his cousin Ambrose grew more and more angrily excited. When challenged he said he had remained silent for otherwise he would have shouted. He adopted a similar style in politics.

Baldwin built and retained the credibility with the public, which is perhaps a politician's most indispensable asset. People believed he was, as the *Manchester Guardian* wrote in a review of one volume of speeches, a 'representative Englishman', or at least 'representative of much that many Englishmen would like themselves to be, but seldom are'.[3] His political character, like the writing in a stick of rock, ran through his private life as much as his public. He refused, for example, to allow his son Oliver to be alienated, even at the cost of accepting Oliver's (at that time illegal) homosexuality and incorporated his partner, John Boyce, into the family. The ordinariness of his public image was reflected in his private correspondence, where he often wrote of feeling humble, or being humbled, in the face of his responsibilities, a word he used in the Christian sense not of inferiority but of being free from the sin of pride, a vessel for God's will. He also talked of 'piety', which he defined as *the gift of reverence for all things that are good, and the gift of performing your duty primarily to those amongst whom you live, and through them to your country and the world ... .* His private life reflected the precepts he advocated in public. Embarrassed by the wartime profits of E P & W Baldwin Ltd that had come so easily when so many men, younger than he was, were sacrificing their lives, he gave away to various charities and the Treasury, a total of about £200,000. (Using HM Treasury's 'Historic Money' table for August 2005, about £6 million at today's prices. I have taken a multiplier of 30. The rate fluctuated greatly during this period so it is only an approximation of the value of Baldwin's charity. By his reckoning it was about a quarter of his fortune.) In a note written in 1938

Baldwin described this divesting of wealth as if *I had pulled my sweater off for a race*. In the same note he emphasised how his religious faith and his sense of *an incessant search for God's will*[4] had directed his efforts. He was religious by upbringing and inclination, a romantic in his literary tastes, but his experience in childhood and until middle age was, in contrast, that of a successful businessman.

Baldwin was no utopian, yet he conveyed an underlying idealism, a commitment to service. After he had won his first election, in 1924, he later told the Swedish ambassador in an extraordinarily intimate and revealing conversation, he felt [I] *was henceforth* [my] *complete self and knew that what had been instilled in* [my] *childhood had now come to life and found an outlet ... I give expression, in some unaccountable way, to what the English people think. For some reason that appeals to me and gives me strength ... The members of the Government know that if I were to go to the polls alone without their support I should nevertheless have the game in my hands.*[5] He was particularly dismissive of political colleagues who sought short-term gain, who failed to honour their commitments, who made promises they did not intend to keep. In an unguarded interview with *The People* in 1924, he spoke of *the old, dirty kind of politics*; he attributed the Press Barons' dislike of him to his refusal to allow them to dictate to him. Yet he was no simple 'Forrest Gump' of Downing Street. He abhorred plotting, but was not without a constant eye to party advantage. He pursued his objectives with a calculation that his rivals discounted to their cost.

In the new world of mass democracy, Baldwin set out to be, he often said, *a healer*, an agent for unity in the face of a newly-enfranchised working class who might wish to use their new power to challenge the *status quo*. The less often described part of his mission was to reconcile the upper classes and educate them in their own need to change, before they resorted to undemocratic methods themselves.

Equally important in making democracy safe was modernising the Conservative Party, attempting to weld its component parts – the aristocratic organisation with a paternalistic inclination, and the businessman's party of self interest, and the landowners' party of tradition – into a party of all classes and of none, that had the machinery to engage and communicate with the widest possible range of voters. Policy remained a matter for the leadership, but a leadership constrained by a knowledge of what the party's supporters believed themselves and knew would be welcomed in their own localities. He tried, with limited success, to broaden the range of Conservative candidates by ending the obligation to underwrite constituency expenses. He took an interest in the development of Conservative Central Office, and made his closest political associate, Davidson, chairman from 1927 to 1930. Following Labour's example, the party expanded its activities into political education run from a new Conservative training college at Ashridge. A research department was established, much effort went into attracting women party workers and women candidates (with rather more success at the former than the latter) and a Young Britons organisation was set up. Publicity became an important activity that Baldwin was able to exploit in a way that both carried his message to a far wider audience than any of his predecessors can have reached, and successfully established his personality in the public mind. The party invested in a van equipped with a projector that toured the country showing voters specially-shot footage of Baldwin, perhaps in the garden of Downing Street or on the stump in the country, but always articulating his policies in the tones of the ordinary man, aided by the echo in his voice of his Worcestershire origins. *When I broadcast,* he once told

Baldwin and the Media

Baldwin's tenure saw the first media revolution of the century: in 1922 a group of firms manufacturing wireless equipment, established the British Broadcasting Company. One of them, Marconi, had opened a radio station in London earlier that year with the call sign '2LO', and it was from the 2LO studio in Savoy Hill (off the Strand) that the BBC began broadcasting. The company went on air on 14 November at 6 p.m., with the news read by Arthur Burrows.

During the next general election campaign in the autumn of 1924, the party leaders were for the first time invited to make election broadcasts on the BBC and thereby changed the nature of electioneering forever. The two main opponents chose to handle this opportunity in completely different fashions: Ramsay MacDonald decided to broadcast live from a mass meeting in Glasgow. Unfortunately for him, with radio technology being in its infancy, the quality of the reception was so poor that he came across as an inconsequential tub-thumper. In contrast to that, Baldwin 'settled himself comfortably into a chair in the BBC Director-General's office, and spoke softly and reassuringly, immediately establishing a rapport with his listeners. It was the beginning of the extraordinary reputation which he acquired as "Honest Stan", the man who understood and was deeply involved in the concerns of the man in the street. Baldwin was a natural broadcaster' (Dick Leonard, *A Century of Premiers* [Palgrave Macmillan, London: 2005] p 119) and set a standard for his successors or anybody who aspired to high elected office: from that moment onwards the party leaders had not only to be effective parliamentarians, but also able to communicate with the electorate through this new medium. The result of the 1924 election was the Conservatives winning an absolute majority with 412 seats, Baldwin becoming Prime Minister, and the first Director-General of the BBC, John Reith, being given the seal of approval for his concept of public service broadcasting, when the company received a royal charter in 1927 as the British Broadcasting Corporation. Its expenses were to be met by a licence fee, paid by anyone owning a radio, and fixed by Baldwin's government at ten shillings.

Walter Citrine, *I always go along at crawling pace so that people can not only hear plainly, but can take it in as I go along.*[6]

His ability to communicate, however, rested on more than his distaste for the intellectual and his representation of the common man. He introduced the electorate to a kind of Conservatism that far outlived his own period in power. *Every future Government must be socialistic*, he averred to the man from *The People* in May 1924, before artlessly claiming ignorance of what socialism was. No more vested interests, he declared. *If we are to live as a party we must live for the people in the widest sense.* Baldwin borrowed the then unfamiliar phrase to speak of a 'property-owning democracy'; he stressed the importance of home ownership in encouraging self-reliance, he toyed with ideas of worker share ownership as an alternative to nationalisation. He warned against talking up the class war, and he smothered his party's appetite for restoring the power of the Lords to block legislation. He recognised the parity of the Dominions with Britain, and he set in motion – against bitter internal opposition – the process of Indian self-rule. It was Baldwin's Conservative Party that accepted and then adapted to the post-war settlement in the 1940s, and it was a disciple of Baldwin's, Rab Butler, who was the chief architect of a transformation that lasted until Margaret Thatcher became leader with support from the neo-liberal wing of the party that Baldwin had suppressed.

The purpose and direction of change in the Conservative Party was driven by his understanding of Labour's appeal. Unlike many Conservatives of his generation, Baldwin saw that Labour was more than the voice of the trade union movement. Increasingly it was the party of modernisation, a party that spoke of peace and rights and idealism in contrast to Tory self-interest and pragmatism. It must be acknowledged as such and treated as a partner in the shared enterprise of keeping democracy in good health. The utopianism of its followers must be respected: the parliamentary ethic of its leaders must be encouraged. The masses must be taught to understand that it was in the nation's advantage that they saw through demagoguery and rejected democratic tyranny, and learned to recognise, as well as their right to power, their duty to exercise it for the whole nation. In all of this, he claimed at the end of his life, he had made a difference.

In the aftermath of the General Strike, industrial relations improved. There were fewer working days lost to strike action in the decade from 1927–37 than at any other time in the 20th century. The Mond-Turner talks attempted to set up a framework to resolve disputes before they became strikes. The General Secretary of the TUC, Walter Citrine, professionalised and reformed the TUC into an organisation capable of contributing to the corporate state of the 1950s. Of course, many of these changes would have happened without Baldwin. Even before 1926, Ernest Bevin of the Transport and General Workers' Union had been thinking of ways of improving understanding between workers and employers. Citrine was responding to trade unions' ambitions for more concerted action when he began strengthening the TUC's bureaucracy. Above all, industrial militancy was first sapped by the defeat of the General Strike and then almost destroyed by the slump. But Baldwin contributed to a climate that made co-operation possible.

Unemployment, sometimes nudging three million, did not fall below one and a half million from 1928 to 1940. Baldwin, like most Conservative politicians of his time, was ignorant of the reality of the lives of millions of British families. He did not see a slum until 1925, and did not travel to the depressed areas of South Wales until he had retired from public life. He knew little or nothing of the harshness of the life, the grimness of the work or the terrible poverty of unemployment of millions of the people whom he aspired to lead. But under his leadership, the Conservative party did come to accept a widening of the obligation of the state to promote the well-being of the people. He encouraged the idea of trade unions as partners in management with an important role in a pluralistic democracy. By defining Conservatives as the national party, the party of peace and comradeship, he offered an alternative to theories of class war. He spoke up not for strikers but for those who suffered because of strike action. In the 1930s, as Oswald Mosley's Blackshirts (and various other Brownshirts) threatened communal peace in the East End of London, and Communist Redshirts prepared to resist them, Baldwin outlawed the wearing of uniforms.

In opposition in the Commons Baldwin established a shadow cabinet that, particularly in his first period in opposition, oversaw the development of a programme for government which embodied what his internal critics considered Tory socialism. But in Baldwin's period as leader, less than three years were spent in opposition. Renewal in government, that most elusive of objectives, was much harder. In government, the politicians had official advice and committees. An Economic Advisory Committee, an early think-tank, was set up. But nothing emerged from either government or the party machine that rivalled Lloyd George's 'Yellow Book', and once those ideas of massive public works and the creation or rejuvenation of a modern national infrastructure – which were brutally discounted by Whitehall – had been taken up by a politician Baldwin thought for most of his career little better than a charlatan, it was unthinkable for Conservatives to embrace them. When, in the mid 1930s, it seemed some rapprochement with Lloyd George was possible, Neville Chamberlain vetoed it.

It was from his reputation as a parliamentarian that much of Baldwin's strength derived. The hours spent listening to his colleagues and opponents from the Treasury bench; the informal conversations with Labour MPs, the encouragement of the younger members and his ability to judge the mood of the House gave him a control that even when it faltered was sustained by the sympathy earned by the unfailingly courteous and genial style. To the end, he retained an extraordinary capacity, under the heaviest duress, to deliver a speech that silenced his critics. His skill in the Commons shored up his position in his own party. In the early 1930s, at a time when away from Parliament the left was arguing for a dictatorship so that Socialism could triumph, and the Parliamentary Labour Party was reduced to a rump of 51 MPs, he consciously tried to keep a place for their return by ensuring that the opposition was not crushed or ignored, but granted proper respect. There is certainly some truth in his friends' claim that his conduct in the Commons made possible the return of a parliamentary socialist party after 1935, and its ultimate victory in 1945. However, the far greater contribution was made by forces within the Labour party itself, against an internal opposition that never came close to commanding a majority. What was more significant was that Baldwin never dismissed or ridiculed Labour to a wider public; he treated the leaders of the whole Labour movement with respect and, through, for example, appointments of their leaders to serve on official committees, he encouraged the involvement of the moderates in public life. *Never try to score off the Labour Party, or to be smart at their expense*, he told a gathering of junior ministers in his final year. *Never do anything to increase the sense of bitterness between the parties in Parliament. Never go out of your way to irritate or anger the Labour Party. Remember that one day we may need them.*[7] Almost his final act as Prime Minister, convinced that Labour members were suffering real hardship, was to double MPs' pay from £200 to £400 a year (£7,000 to £14,000). He introduced a salary for the Leader of the Opposition so that he would not need to indulge in what he felt was potentially corrupting work outside Parliament, and he increased ministerial salaries.

Yet, partly because he sometimes thought it strategically wiser to give in to his party, the picture of the healer and unifier is not wholly consistent. In 1924, he taunted Labour with the Zinoviev letter, a move he subsequently justified by the conviction that it had been genuine. His private correspondence indicates that he felt MacDonald had failed to challenge the extreme left in the party, while the security services painted a lurid picture of infiltration in the wider Labour movement that was ruthlessly exploited by ministers in the run up to the General Strike. During the strike, Churchill came perilously close to provoking violence, although the licence he was allowed probably served as a safety-valve for the party die-hards while its intemperate tone robbed it of much of its power. However, it was royal opposition that prevented a repetition of the statement that troops could take any means necessary to protect supplies, and it was the King and civil servants together who prevented Churchill legislating to stop trade unions accessing their own funds for strike pay. Despite making one of his most memorable speeches in opposition to trade union legislation in 1925, Baldwin felt too weak to block it in 1927. In that year he also authorised the Arcos raid, a gesture that was less a contribution to national security than it was a sop to party opinion. He was a man, A J P Taylor thought, of soft words and hard actions. The paradox was repeated: he was a shy and private individual, yet he could inspire thousands of strangers with a simple phrase. He used personal electoral success to dominate his party, and on the occasions when he set an objective, pursued it with a hard-headed clarity of purpose that rarely failed to overcome opposition. By defining mass democracy in such a way that a majority of the country could accept it, he enabled a transformation of Britain's political culture to take place, a seismic shift in its centre of gravity and its dominant concerns, in which Labour became a party of power in the safe embrace of a two-party system.

'History will judge us kindly', Churchill told Roosevelt and Stalin at the Tehran Conference in 1943; when asked how he could be so sure, he responded: 'because I shall write the history.'[8] Churchill blamed Baldwin as the leader whose inertia had nearly cost Britain her freedom and it is a version of history that through vigorous repetition and a basis in truth has become almost beyond revision. The following facts are true: Baldwin was closely involved in the development of foreign and defence policy from 1932 onwards. By 1932 Britain's defence spending had reached a point so low that the infrastructure of skilled men and industrial plant began to disintegrate, accelerating a trend caused by the slump. The failure to invest adequately then made later rearmament slower and more difficult than it would otherwise have been. There was a case for large-scale rearmament from the moment Hitler took power in 1933 committed to treaty revision. By 1936, the state of Britain's defences made it impossible to conduct diplomacy that might end in European war. Baldwin allowed Neville Chamberlain's concern for the economic circumstances and desire to avoid borrowing to slow the rearmament effort. He refused to sanction the militarisation of some parts of British industry.

But so are these: Britain was nearly bankrupt in 1931. She was still repaying debt incurred in the First World War in 1934. Rearming could have put at risk the revival of an economy where two million people were unemployed. By-elections showed a popular reluctance to risk war; an arms race was considered likely to provoke one. The Peace Ballot in 1934–5 was taken as confirmation of this mood. Germany had been completely disarmed in the aftermath of the First World War and consequently began rearming from a much lower base than Britain. The 1935 general election, although Baldwin subsequently claimed it as a mandate for rearmament, was fought on the promise of 'no great armaments' and of a defence programme that would enable Britain to fulfil her obligations in the name of collective security. Faith in the League of Nations grew in inverse proportion to the likelihood of its achieving its mission as a force for world peace. There was good reason for Baldwin to doubt France's appetite for war, particularly against Italy. After the Franco-Soviet pact, he was alarmed by the risk of being drawn into war on the same side as Russia. Although it was agreed that Hitler was 'mad' and unstable, it was not certain that he wanted war and it was judged impolitic to make pacific overtures at the same time as turning the economy over to a war footing. It was also respectable to argue that to move against either Italy or Germany individually would encourage them to move closer together, at the cost of Austrian independence and at further threat to France. War would unavoidably have involved the whole of Europe. Churchill, who as Chancellor had been a notable cutter of defence budgets, had been wrong about the imminent Bolshevik threat, the conduct of the General Strike, self-government for India and, at least in the public mind, the Abdication. He further damaged his political credibility by working with Baldwin's enemies in the press.

To rearm at the rate that Churchill was urging would have been an extraordinary political risk that would have appeared to many in Britain and in Europe as a deliberately provocative act. Yet in Germany's volatile domestic politics, it might have led to Hitler being deposed, or at least contained and deterred. What is clear, however, is that Baldwin was himself persuaded of the need to rearm at least by 1934, if not earlier, as he told Churchill at their private meeting in July 1936. He said he was held back by the need to bring the electorate with him. The alternative to a Conservative government was indeed a pacifist, disarming, Labour one; but Labour was such a broken force after 1931 that the prospect of a Conservative defeat can never have been a serious consideration, and after a second triumph in 1935 was out of the question for another parliamentary term. In Baldwin's defence, it can be argued that he feared ideology more than armaments. The totalitarians' ability to capture hearts and minds was more dangerous even than their armies. Rearmament had to have national support; it must not be seen – as the Left was claiming – to be a move towards Fascism by the governing classes. Above all, the country had to believe that democracy itself was an ideal for which any sacrifice would be justified. Baldwin was sometimes guilty of sentimentality. He appears to have underestimated the potential to lead people from the front as well as to educating them. Popular support was an important source of his power, particularly after the overt machinations against him of 1930–1 which were followed by the extraordinary popular triumph for the national government at the end of 1931. It was not, or not only, personal advantage, however. The idea that he spoke for England was a mainspring of his actions, and until 1935 England did not yet understand the need to rearm. He could not, therefore, authorise such a move until he had convinced the voters that it was an unavoidable necessity. *A democracy is two years behind a dictatorship*, Baldwin repeated again and again. To the deputation of July 1936, he had said, *I have never quite seen the clear line by which you can approach people to scare them but not scare them into fits …*[9]

Baldwin himself was appalled at the idea of another war, a war that he warned would end civilisation, destroying democracy as it destroyed lives and property. By the summer of 1936 he was on the edge of a nervous breakdown. He retreated for nearly three months, returning to the Abdication crisis. Yet even in the final months of his time in office, he was supporting Chamberlain against the more militaristic urgings of his young friend and Foreign Secretary, Anthony Eden. Baldwin was an old man: 68 when he became Prime Minister for the third time. He was tired. He, who had never relished public life, had been at the forefront of national politics for nearly 20 years. Emotionally, he began handing over to Chamberlain long before he retired. But his failure to press for rearmament, or to pursue it vigorously once the course was set, goes beyond the conciliatory tendencies of an old man on the brink of retirement, to the heart of his leadership style.

'The legacy of Baldwinism is incompetence, because of his sentimental all-men-are-brothers-so-don't-let-us-wrangle attitude,'[10] Churchill said in a typical piece of hyperbole. Baldwin did not imagine conflict could always be avoided. Nonetheless, to avoid it was his purpose in politics. Conflict, or preparing for conflict, was not an objective he willingly embraced; in the 1930s, amid the complications of an infant economic recovery and conflicting advice about how best to handle Germany, it required an appetite for administration and a driving determination that Baldwin would never claim for himself. The time lost as a result of his inadequate political energy might have made the difference between victory and defeat in the years ahead – had not the nation's capacity to stand together lent a resilience that was to become an indispensable adjunct to military capacity. Churchill's approach, from a sworn enemy of the left, might have secured the nation's defences but at the expense of national unity. Britain has less to blame Baldwin for than it had to thank him.

The post-war myths have served their purpose. In 2006, when the country is again uncertain about its national identity, it is surely time to rediscover a political leader who understood how to persuade a people to believe that the whole is greater than the sum of its parts.

NOTES

Chapter 1: Origins

1. Stanley Baldwin, speech to the Empire Rally of Youth in the Albert Hall, 1937.
2. Quoted in Philip Williams and Edward Baldwin, *Baldwin Papers* (Cambridge University Press, Cambridge: 2004) p 46, hereafter *Baldwin Papers*.
3. K Middlemas and J Barnes, *Baldwin* (Weidenfeld & Nicolson, London: 1969) p 44.
4. 11 February 1917, quoted in *Baldwin Papers*, p 29.
5. 'Religion and National Life', May 1931 in Stanley Baldwin, *This Torch of Freedom* (Hodder & Stoughton, London: 1937) p 84.
6. G M Young, *Stanley Baldwin* (Rupert Hart Davis, London: 1952) p 19.
7. Philip Williamson, *Stanley Baldwin* (Cambridge University Press, London: 1999) p 97.
8. Williamson, *Stanley Baldwin*, p 121. This is essential reading, if only as a masterly corrective to earlier biographies.
9. Middlemas and Barnes, *Baldwin*, p 41.
10. Count Palmestierna's memoir, Appendix C, *Baldwin Papers*, p 497.
11. Reproduced in *Baldwin Papers*, p 23.
12. Quoted in *Baldwin Papers*, p 22.
13. Speech quoted in Middlemas and Barnes, *Baldwin*, p 54.
14. Quoted in Williamson, *Stanley Baldwin*, p 136.

Chapter 2: If you can wait ... (1922–4)

1. August 1938 note 'for cousin', in *Baldwin Papers*, p 454.
2. 1918 election results: Coalition Unionist 335 MPs, Coalition Liberal 133, Coalition Lab 10, Conservative 23, Liberal 28, Labour 63, Others 90.
3. Austin Chamberlain letter 11 October 1922, quoted in Maurice Cowling, *The Impact of Labour 1920–1924* (Cambridge University Press, Cambridge: 1971) p 181.

4. Robert Rhodes James (ed), *Memoirs of a Conservative, J C C Davidson's Memoirs and Papers, 1910–1937* (Weidenfeld & Nicolson, London: 1969) p 112.

5. See Cowling, *The Impact of Labour 1920–1924*, p162

6. Letter of 29 September 1922 to Mimi Davidson, quoted in *Baldwin Papers*, pp 69–70.

7. Quoted in Middlemas and Barnes, *Baldwin*, p 115.

8. Rt Hon Arthur Griffith-Boscawen (1865–1946), then a stolid Agriculture Minister.

9. For the full speech see G M Young, *Stanley Baldwin*, pp 40–2.

10. Liberal MP and Chancellor, 1915–16, but in 1922 Chairman of the Midland Bank.

11. Rhodes James (ed), *Memoirs of a Conservative*, p 118.

12. Cowling, *The Impact of Labour 1920–1924*, p 202.

Chapter 3: If you can dream … (1923– 4)

1. Baldwin to the Swedish Ambassador, Count Palmestierna, Baldwin Papers, p 496.

2. See 'Arketall' in Harold Nicolson, *Some People* (Constable, London: 1927) for a hilarious but not unkind description of his character.

3. J C C Davidson (1889–1970), 1st Viscount Davidson 1937. Married Joan 'Mimi' Dickinson, Baldwin's devoted walking companion.

4. G M Young, *Stanley Baldwin*, p 56.

5. G M Young, *Stanley Baldwin*, p 42.

6. G M Young, *Stanley Baldwin*, p 58.

7. Roy Jenkins, *Baldwin* (Collins: 1987) p 66.

8. *Baldwin Papers*, p 85.

9. *Baldwin Papers*, p 98.

10. Williamson, *Stanley Baldwin*, p 143.

11. From the Keynes Papers, quoted in Robert Skidelsky, *John Maynard Keynes* (one volume edition, Macmillan, London: 2003) p 370.

12. 19 July 1923, quoted in Middlemas and Barnes, *Baldwin*, p 170.

13. 5.2 million voted in the second 1910 election; 10.7 million in 1918 and 14 million in 1922. Figures from David Butler and Gareth Butler (eds), *Twentieth Century British Political Facts* (Palgrave, London: 2000).

14. Austen Chamberlain memorandum given in *Baldwin Papers*, p 127.

15. G M Young, *Stanley Baldwin*, p 62.
16. G M Young, *Stanley Baldwin*, p 57.
17. Jenkins, *Baldwin*, p 70.
18. Middlemas and Barnes, *Baldwin*, p 229.
19. Middlemas and Barnes, *Baldwin*, p 241.
20. Conservatives 258, Liberal 159, Labour 191, Others 7.
21. Quoted in Middlemas and Barnes, *Baldwin*, p 251.
22. 'You forbore to take advantage of [my inexperience] and you gave me a lesson by which I hope I shall profit in the years to come.' Letter to Asquith, October 1926, *Baldwin Papers*, p 192.
23. Stamfordham memorandum for the King, quoted in *Baldwin Papers*, p 159.
24. Quoted in Middlemas and Barnes, *Baldwin*, p 2.
25. November 1923, quoted in Williamson, *Stanley Baldwin*, p 214.
26. Quoted in Middlemas and Barnes, *Baldwin*, p 274.
27. Conservative 419 MPs, Liberal 40, Labour 151, Communist 1, Others 4.

Chapter 4: Triumph (1924– 6)

1. Verse given to Baldwin by Kipling on Christmas Morning 1924, quoted in Williamson, *Stanley Baldwin*, p 167.
2. An expression, with its implication of awe, that Baldwin later denied using.
3. Quoted in Robert Skidelsky, *John Maynard Keynes, The Economist as Saviour 1920 –1937* (Macmillan, London: 1992) p 198.
4. From *Baldwin Papers*, p 493.
5. Hansard, 6 March 1925, quoted in Middlemas and Barnes, *Baldwin*, p 297.
6. WSC V/1 quoted in *Baldwin Papers*, p 169.
7. 'The Economic Consequences of Mr Churchill' quoted in Skidelsky, *John Maynard Keynes, The Economist as Saviour 1920–1937*, p 204.
8. Birmingham speech, 5 March 1925 quoted in *Baldwin Papers*, p 196.
9. Letter to a deputation of churchmen, 19 July 1926, quoted in *Baldwin Papers*, p 184.
10. Baldwin to Curzon, January 1925, Curzon papers F112/324, quoted in *Baldwin Papers*, p 168.

11. Hansard, 2 May 1926, quoted in Middlemas and Barnes, *Baldwin*, p 411.
12. For the most recent account of the strike, which draws on newly-released documents in the Public Record Office, see Anne Perkins, *A Very British Strike* (Macmillan, London: 2005).
13. Letter to a deputation of churchmen, 19 July 1926, quoted in *Baldwin Papers*, p 186.
14. 5 September 1926 letter to Winston Churchill, Churchill papers, CHAR 22/112/78; WSC V/1 pp 773–4, quoted in *Baldwin Papers*, p 190.
15. Arthur Jenkins, who became an MP, was arrested during the Strike after an improbable dust-up with the police. It appears he had become trapped between rival factions. But it added greatly to his credibility in later life.
16. To Lady Londonderry, 27 December 1924, quoted in *Baldwin Papers*, p 167.

Chapter 5: Disaster (1926–31)

1. Verse of election song emanating from Conservative Central Office, 1929.
2. Speech to the Primrose League, 2 May 1924 quoted in Williamson, *Stanley Baldwin*, p 152. This section relies heavily on Mr Williamson's discussion of Baldwin's political purpose.
3. 1 May 1925, letter to Joan Davidson, quoted in *Baldwin Papers*, p 171.
4. Stuart Hibberd, 'This is – London', quoted in Kenneth Young, *Baldwin* (Weidenfeld & Nicolson, London: 1976) p 47.
5. Letter to 2nd Earl of Litton, in Baldwin Papers, p 203.
6. Rhodes James (ed), *Memoirs of a Conservative*, p 197.
7. Many editions, first published 1955.
8. From *Baldwin Papers*, p 205.
9. *Baldwin Papers*, p 220.
10. To Oliver Baldwin, 8 June 1929, in *Baldwin Papers*, p 222.
11. To Sir John Simon, 19 February 1930, from *Baldwin Papers*, p 227.
12. See below next chapter.
13. Lytton to Irwin, 9–10 November 1929, in *Baldwin Papers*, p 224.

Chapter 6: Worn-out Tools (1931–7)

1. See Jenkins, *Baldwin*, in particular Chapter Six, 'The National Government'.
2. See letter from Sir Edward Grenfell to J P Morgan, 14 August 1931, in *Baldwin Papers*, p 261.
3. To Lucy from the Ritz, Paris, 22 August 1931, in *Baldwin Papers*, p 265.
4. Dawson Memorandum, 23 August 1931, in *Baldwin Papers*, p 266.
5. Page Croft, 26 August 1931, in *Baldwin Papers*, p 269.
6. Robert Skidelsky, *John Maynard Keynes 1883–1946* (Macmillan, London: 2003) p 477.
7. P Snowden, 'Autobiography, II', quoted in Charles Mowat, *Britain Between the Wars 1928–1940* (Methuen, London: 1955) p 419.
8. Partly reprinted in A J P Taylor (ed), *Off the Record: Political Interviews 1933–1943* (Hutchinson, London: 1973) and quoted in Baldwin Papers, p 317.
9. Quoted in Middlemas and Barnes, *Baldwin*, p 689.
10. Also quoted in Middlemas and Barnes, *Baldwin*, p 689.

Chapter 7: Nerve and Sinew (1931–7)

1. See Butler and Butler (eds), *Twentieth Century British Political Facts*, pp 422–3.
2. Properly known as the Business Committee.
3. Memorandum of a visit paid by Baldwin. R A Butler papers, G6/57 quoted in Baldwin Papers, p 335. Interesting description of Baldwin's personal style.
4. Hansard, 10 November 1932.
5. Harold Nicolson, *King George V* (Constable, London: 1952) p 528.
6. Widely quoted in e.g. Kenneth Young, *Baldwin*, p 112, but not in Davidson's own Memoirs at this date, although the sentiment is repeated in 1936.
7. A phrase that Tony Blair came close to using himself in defence of his determination to invade Iraq in 2003.
8. Robert Rhodes James, *Anthony Eden* (Weidenfeld & Nicolson, London: 1986) p 157.
9. Rhodes James, *Anthony Eden*, p 163.
10. 28 July 1936, PREM1/193/102-93 quoted in *Baldwin Papers*, p 374.

11. 16 July 1936, Nigel Nicolson (ed), *Harold Nicolson, Diaries & Letters 1930–39* (Collins, London: 1966) p 263.
12. Nigel Nicolson (ed), *Harold Nicolson, Diaries & Letters 1930–39*, p 272.

Chapter 8: Or walk with Kings: The Abdication Crisis 1936
1. SB Speech, 3 May 1935 quoted in G M Young, *Stanley Baldwin*, p 232.
2. Harold Nicolson, *King George V*, p 462.
3. From Middlemas and Barnes, *Baldwin*, p 905.
4. 30 November 1936, Nigel Nicolson (ed), *Harold Nicolson, Diaries & Letters 1930–39*, p 274.
5. Quoted in Andrew Roberts, *'The Holy Fox': A Biography of Lord Halifax* (Weidenfeld & Nicolson, London: 1991) p 61.
6. From Lucy Baldwin's diary, quoted in Middlemas and Barnes, *Baldwin*, p 1004.
7. Nigel Nicolson (ed), *Harold Nicolson, Diaries & Letters 1930–39*, p 280.
8. *The Times*, 28 May 1937, quoted in Middlemas and Barnes, *Baldwin*, p 1039.

Chapter 9: The Baldwin Era
1. 23 April 1937, 'Mr Baldwin's Testament', from *Baldwin Papers*, p 433.
2. Keith Feiling: Toryism: A Political Dialogue. Quoted by David Willetts MP in a speech 'New Conservatism for a New Century' in June 2005.
3. Quoted on the jacket of 4th edition of Stanley Baldwin, *This Torch of Freedom* (Hodder & Stoughton, London: 1937) (first published 1935).
4. Note for cousin, August 1938, in *Baldwin Papers*, p 454.
5. *Baldwin Papers*, p 497.
6. *Baldwin Papers*, p 386.
7. Ben Pimlott (ed), *The Political Diary of Hugh Dalton* (Jonathan Cape, London: 1986) p 205.
8. Martin Gilbert, *Winston Churchill, The Wilderness Years* (Macmillan, London: 1981).
9. *Baldwin Papers*, p 378.
10. Gilbert, *Winston Churchill, The Wilderness Years*, p 176.

CHRONOLOGY

Year	Premiership

1923   British Prime Minister Andrew Bonar Law resigns due to ill health.
22 May: Stanley Baldwin becomes Prime Minister, aged 55.
Conservatives lose heavily in general election.

1924   12 January: Baldwin leaves No 10 Downing Street for the first time.
In ten speeches, Baldwin shores up leadership and sets out purpose
of Conservative party for 20th century.
Parliament is dissolved following defeat of Labour on question of
prosecution of the acting editor of *Workers' Weekly* for inciting
soldiers to mutiny.
British Foreign Office publishes Zinoviev Letter, apparently
inciting revolutionary activity in the army and Ireland.
October: Baldwin becomes Prime Minister for second time, with
his own mandate on programme of 'social idealism tied to sound
finance'.

1925   Churchill, Chancellor of the Exchequer, returns £ to Gold Standard
at pre-war parity. Keynes warns of deflationary impact on pay.
Also leads to tight constraints on defence budget
July: 'Red Friday' when government capitulates to threats of general
strike and pays subsidy to support miners' pay.

History	Culture
French and Belgian troops occupy the Ruhr when Germany fails to make reparation payments.	François Mauriac, *Genitrix.*
The USSR formally comes into existence.	P G Wodehouse, *The Inimitable Jeeves.*
Severe earthquake in Japan destroys all of Yokohama and most of Tokyo.	Edna St Vincent Millay, *The Ballad of the Harp-Weaver; A Few Figs from Thistles.*
Miguel Primo de Rivera assumes dictatorship of Spain.	Martin Buber, *I and Thou.*
Wilhelm Marx succeeds Stresemann as German Chancellor.	Sigmund Freud, *The Ego and the Id.*
	Max Beckmann, *The Trapeze.*
State of Emergency declared in Germany.	Mark Chagall, *Love Idyll.*
British Mandate in Palestine begins.	George Gershwin, *Rhapsody in Blue.*
Adolf Hitler's *coup d'état* (The Beer Hall Putsch) fails.	Bela Bartok, *Dance Suite.*
	BBC listings magazine *Radio Times* first published.
Death of Lenin.	Noel Coward, *The Vortex.*
Turkish national assembly expels the Ottoman dynasty.	E M Forster, *A Passage to India.*
Greece is proclaimed a republic.	Thomas Mann, *The Magic Mountain.*
Nazi Party enters the Reichstag with 32 seats for the first time, after the elections to the German parliament.	George Bernard Shaw, *St Joan.*
	'The Blue Four' expressionist group is formed.
Calvin Coolidge, Republican, wins US Presidential Election.	George Braque, *Sugar Bowl.*
	Fernand Leger, *Ballet Mecanique.*
	King George V makes first royal radio broadcast, opening the British Empire Exhibition at Wembley.
Christiania, the Norwegian capital, is renamed Oslo.	Noel Coward, *Hay Fever.*
	Franz Kafka, *The Trial.*
In Italy, Mussolini announces that he will take dictatorial powers.	Virginia Woolf, *Mrs Dalloway.*
	Pablo Picasso, *Three Dancers.*
Paul von Hindenburg, former military leader, is elected President of Germany.	Marc Chagall, *The Drinking Green Pig.*
Hitler reorganises Nazi Party.	Lyonel Feininger, *Tower.*
	Alban Berg, *Wozzek.*
Locarno conference discusses the question of a security pact. Locarno Treaty later signed in London.	Ferruccio Busconi, *Doctor Faust.*
	Film: *Battleship Potemkin.*

Year	Premiership

1926 3–12 May :General Strike in support of miners' pay claim
After government victory, Baldwin brings back eight-hour day in
  pits, seen as vindictive

1927 Trade Disputes bill ends contracting-out and outlaws strikes
  threatening the state.
Baldwin travels to Canada with the Prince of Wales.
India Commission under Sir John Simon established to review
  Montagu-Chelmsford Act.

History	Culture
Germany applies for admission to League of Nations but is blocked by Spain and Brazil.	Franz Kafka, *The Castle.*
France proclaims the Lebanon as a republic.	A A Milne, *Winnie the Pooh.*
Germany is admitted into the League of Nations; as a result, Spain leaves.	Ernest Hemingway, *The Sun Also Rises.*
Fascist youth organisation Ballilla in Italy and Hitlerjugend in Germany are founded.	Sean O'Casey, *The Plough and The Stars.*
Imperial Conference in London, decides that Britain and the Dominions are autonomous communities, equal in status.	Oscar Kokoschka, *Terrace in Richmond.*
In the USSR, Trotsky and Zinoviev are expelled from Politburo of Communist Party, following Stalin's victory.	Edvard Munch, *The Red House.*
	Eugene D'Albert, *The Golem.*
	Puccini, *Turandot.*
	Film: *The General.*
Inter-Allied military control of Germany ends.	Marcel Proust, *Le Temps retrouve.*
'Black Friday' in Germany – the economic system collapses.	Virginia Woolf, *To the Lighthouse.*
Britain recognises rule of Ibn Saud in the Hejaz.	Jean Cocteau, *Orphee* and *Oedipe-Roi.*
President Hindenburg of Germany repudiates Germany's responsibility for the First World War.	Hermann Hesse, *Steppenwolf.*
Trotsky and Zinoviev are ultimately expelled from the Communist Party.	Adolf Hitler, *Mein Kampf.*
Britain recognises Iraq's independence and promises to support its application for membership of the League of Nations.	Martin Heidegger, *Sein und Zeit.*
	Bach, *The Art of the Fugue.*
	George Gershwin, *Funny Face.*
	George Bracque, *Glass and Fruit.*
	Edward Hopper, *Manhattan Bridge.*
	Film: *The Jazz Singer.*

Year	Premiership

1928 Lloyd George's 'Yellow Book' makes radical proposals for dealing with the Depression and unemployment.

1929 Irwin tells Baldwin Dominion status for India essential amid fears of terrible communal violence.

'Safety First' election campaign built round Baldwin himself ends in failure.

4 June: Baldwin leaves office a second time.

History	Culture
Transjordan becomes self-governing under the British Mandate.	D H Lawrence, *Lady Chatterley's Lover.*
Italian electorate is reduced from ten million to three million.	Aldous Huxley, *Point Counterpoint.*
Herman Müller is appointed German Chancellor.	Max Beckmann, *Black Lillies.* Henri Matisse, *Seated Odalisque.*
Kellogg-Briand Pact outlawing war and providing for peaceful settlement of disputes, is signed.	George Gershwin, *An American in Paris.*
Herbert Hoover elected US President.	Kurt Weill, *The Threepenny Opera.*
Dominion Status voted for India.	
Albania is proclaimed a Kingdom.	
Plebiscite in Germany against building new battleships fails.	
Alexander Fleming discovers Penicillin.	
Dictatorship is established in Yugoslavia under King Alexander I; constitution is suppressed.	Jean Cocteau, *Les Enfants Terribles.*
St Valentines Day Massacre of Chicago gangsters.	Ernest Hemingway, *A Farewell to Arms.*
Fascists win single-party elections in Italy.	Erich Remarque, *All Quiet on the Western Front.*
Germany accepts Young Plan at Reparations Conference in the Hague – Allies agree to evacuate the Rhineland.	Chagall, *Love Idyll.* Piet Mondrian, *Composition with Yellow and Blue.*
Arabs attack Jews in Palestine following dispute over Jewish use of Wailing Wall.	Museum of Modern Art New York opens.
US stock exchange collapses, world economic crisis begins. Cessation of loans to Europe.	Heidegger, *What is Philosophy?* Noel Coward, *Bittersweet.*
Britain resumes relations with the USSR.	

1935   George V's Silver Jubilee

Ailing MacDonald resigns after passage of Government of India Act on which he and Baldwin have worked together.

June: Peace Ballot indicates massive support for League of Nations and disarmament.

7 June: Baldwin returns to office a third time as head of a National Government.

November: General Election and another landslide for the National Government/Conservatives which Baldwin treats as mandate for rearmament.

December: Baldwin's close political ally, Sam Hoare, as Foreign Secretary, negotiates Hoare-Laval pact with France dismembering Abyssinia and undermines League of Nations. Uproar forces Hoare's resignation. Sanctions are applied but have no effect.

Baldwin makes disastrous 'lips are sealed' speech

1936   January: George V dies: Baldwin's broadcast on occasion of King's death another personal triumph.

March: Churchill passed over for new role of Minister for Defence in favour of Sir Thomas Inskip.

Major programmes of social reform, largely guided by Neville Chamberlain as Chancellor, instigated. School leaving age raised to 15, slum clearance begun, unemployment benefit reformed (not successfully). Public Order Act outlaws wearing of political uniforms.

Baldwin hopes Hitler will fight in the East rather than the West.

From June onwards is showing signs of severe nervous strain. Takes August – October off for complete rest.

October: start of Abdication crisis as Edward VIII's mistress, Wallis Simpson, divorces husband.

December: Edward VIII abdicates in order to marry Mrs Simpson.

History	Culture
Anglo-Indian trade pact signed.	Karl Barth, *Credo.*
Saarland is incorporated into Germany following a plebiscite.	*Brockhaus Encyclopaedia* completed.
Prime Ministers of Italy, France and Britain issue protest at German rearmament and agree to act together against Germany.	George Gershwin, *Porgy and Bess.*
	Richard Strauss, *Die Schweigsame Frau.*
	T S Eliot, *Murder in the Cathedral.*
Hitler announces anti-Jewish 'Nuremberg Laws'. Swastika to become Germany's official flag.	Emlyn Williams, *Night Must Fall.*
	Ivy Compton-Burnett, *A House and its Head.*
League of Nations imposes sanctions against Italy following its invasion of Abyssinia.	Films: *The 39 Steps. Top Hat.*

History	Culture
German troops occupy Rhineland, violating Treaty of Versailles.	J M Keynes, *General Theory of Employment, Interest and Money.*
Franco mutiny in Morocco and throughout Spain starting civil war.	A J Ayer, *Language, Truth and Logic.*
British end protectorate over Egypt.	Piet Mondrian, *Composition in Red and Blue.*
Franco appointed nationalist chief of Spanish state.	Prokofiev, *Peter and the Wolf.*
Mosley leads anti-Jewish march in London.	Benny Goodman 'The King of Swing'.
Mussolini proclaims the Rome-Berlin Axis.	Aldous Huxley, *Eyeless in Gaza.*
	Penguin Books starts paperback revolution.
Roosevelt, democrat, re-elected president of the USA.	Berlin Olympics broadcast on TV, Germany wins 33 Gold Medals, USA wins 24.
Germany and Japan sign Anti-Comintern Pact against international communism.	Films: *Modern Times. Camille. The Petrified Forest.*
Amy Johnson flies from England to Cape Town.	BBC begins world's first television transmission service.
Crystal Palace destroyed by fire.	Film: *Things to Come.*

Year	Premiership
1937	May: Coronation of George VI 28 May: Baldwin leaves office, amid glowing notices having served as Prime Minister for all together seven years and 82 days.

History	Culture
Spanish Civil War: Germans bomb Basque capital Guernica.	George Orwell, *The Road to Wigan Pier*.
Airship *Hindenburg* explodes in USA.	Fernand Leger, *Le Transport des Forces*.
Japan invades China, eventually captures Shanghai: Rape of Nanjing (250,000 Chinese killed).	Picasso, *Guernica*.
UK Royal Commission on Palestine recommends partition into British and Arab areas and Jewish state.	Jean-Paul Sartre, *Nausea*.
	John Steinbeck, *Of Mice and Men*.
	Nylon patented in USA.
Italy joins German-Japanese Anti-Comintern Pact.	Films: *Snow White and the Seven Dwarfs*. *A Star is Born*. *La Grande Illusion*.
Irish Free State becomes Eire under de Valera's Irish Constitution.	
Pope Pius XI's message that Nazism is anti-Christian to be announced from all Catholic pulpits in Germany.	
Frank Whittle invents jet engine.	

FURTHER READING

This is the 11th biography of Baldwin; even now, nearly 70 years after his death, he remains a controversial figure. The first three accounts of his life were written during his political career: A G Whyte's *Stanley Baldwin, A Biographical Character Study* (Chapman and Hall, London: 1926), Wickham Steed's *The Real Stanley Baldwin* (Nisbet, London: 1930) and Arthur Bryant, *Stanley Baldwin* (Hamish Hamilton, London: 1937), are hard to find and suffer from the discretion of the time and the weaknesses of biographies published while the subject is still alive. There is also a book by an American writer, Robert Bechhofer, *Stanley Baldwin: Man or Miracle?* published by Greenburg, USA in 1937, which must be worth reading for the title alone.

Baldwin, after some consideration about whether to co-operate at all with a biography, invited G M Young, a young historian and Fellow of All Souls to write his life. Young, who frequently stayed at Astley to talk to the ageing Baldwin and work on his papers, appears not to have liked his subject, or perhaps merely found him intellectually lightweight. He told Roy Jenkins that he found Chamberlain more charming. His *Stanley Baldwin* (Rupert Hart Davis, London: 1952) is short and unsympathetic and – perhaps not surprisingly for a book written in the immediate aftermath of the Second World War – fails to refute Churchill's charge of betrayal. It provoked a short retaliation from D C Somervell, *Stanley Baldwin. An Examination of Some Features of GM Young's biography* (Faber and Faber, London: 1953) and then soon afterwards a biography by his younger son: A W Baldwin, *My Father: the True Story* (Allen and Unwin: 1955) which has a detailed examination and justification of his approach to rearmament.

If Young is short and unkind, the next volume to be published, Keith Middlemas and John Barnes's *Baldwin* (Weidenfeld & Nicolson, London: 1969), is very long and generally sympathetic. Although the whole is hard to digest, no individual event of significance is left unexplored in the thoughtful and intelligent manner of two professional historians. H Montgomery Hyde was an Ulster MP and a professional writer, best known for his work on Oscar Wilde. His *Baldwin, the Unexpected Prime Minister* (Hart-Davis, MacGibbon, London: 1973), is shorter and readable. It was followed by Roy Jenkins, *Baldwin* (Collins, London: 1987) which is elegant as well as readable and studded with the slightly feline observations of a writer who was himself at the summit of the political world for a time. Easily the most stimulating of all is Philip Williamson's *Stanley Baldwin* (Cambridge University Press, Cambridge: 1999) which has since been followed by a selection of documents from Baldwin's own papers as well as letters and diaries from many other collections, edited by Philip Williamson and Baldwin's grandson, the current Earl Baldwin, *The Baldwin Papers* (Cambridge University Press, Cambridge: 2004). These together provide a compelling interpretation of Baldwin's ambition and motivation. For Baldwin in his own words, the *Baldwin Papers* together with collections of his speeches and writings (*On England* [Philip Allan: 1926], *Our Inheritance. Speeches and Addresses* [Hodder & Stoughton, London: 1928], *This Torch of Freedom* [Hodder and Stoughton, London: 1935] and *Service of Our Lives. Last Speeches as Prime Minister 1937* [Hodder & Stoughton, London: 1938]) are invaluable.

Other closely related works include detailed studies such as Maurice Cowling, *The Impact of Labour 1920–1924* (Cambridge University Press, Cambridge: 1971), which although now quite venerable (and an ascerbic contrast with Williamson's work), remains an enlightening study of a watershed in British politics. Another of his works covers the period up to 1940: Maurice Cowling *The Impact of Hitler. British Politics and British Policy 1933–1940* (Cambridge University Press, Cambridge: 1975). Stuart Ball's *Baldwin and the Conservative Party, The Crisis of 1929–1931* (Yale University Press: 1988), examines the years when Baldwin's grip on the leadership nearly slipped, and gives a useful picture of the different influences at play. There is a good, short biographical essay by Lord Blake in *The Baldwin Age*, a collection of essays edited by John Raymond (Eyre & Spottiswood, London: 1960), and of course Blake's history of the Tory Party, Robert Blake, *The Conservative Party from Peel to Thatcher* (Fontana Press, London: 1985) is indispensable. Among other studies of the period Robert Skidelsky's *Politicians and the Slump, The Labour Government of 1929–1931* (Macmillan, London: 1967) is useful. Charles Loch Mowat, *Britain Between the Wars 1928–1940* (Methuen, London: 1955) is a classic and has not yet been replaced. Philip Williamson has also written *National Crisis and National Government. British Politics, the Economy and*

Empire 1926–1932 (Cambridge University Press, Cambridge: 1992). Anne Perkins, *A Very British Strike* (Macmillan, London: 2006), is the latest account of the General Strike, and pays more attention to the politics of the time than earlier ones.

Biographies of other important characters are plentiful. Robert Rhodes James edited *Memoirs of a Conservative, J.C.C. Davidson's Memoirs and Papers, 1910–1937* (Weidenfeld & Nicolson, London: 1969) which is full of insights from someone Baldwin found a loyal and sympathetic ally. The following are also important: David Gilmour's *Curzon* (John Murray, London: 1994), Andrew Roberts's *'The Holy Fox'* (Weidenfeld & Nicolson, London: 1991), Roy Jenkins's *Asquith* (Collins, London: 1964), A J P Taylor, *Beaverbrook* (Hamish Hamilton, London: 1972), Alan Bullock, *The Life and Times of Ernest Bevin, Vol 1 Trade Union Leader* (Heinemann, London: 1960), David Dutton, *Austen Chamberlain: Gentleman in Politics* (Ross Anderson, Bolton: 1985), David Dilks, *Neville Chamberlain, vol 1, 1869–1929* (Cambridge University Press, Cambridge: 1984), Robert Rhodes James, *Churchill: a Study in Failure, 1900–1939* (Weidenfeld & Nicolson, London: 1970), Martin Gilbert, *Winston S. Churchill, vol V, 1922–1939* (Heinemann, London: 1976), Robert Rhodes James, *Anthony Eden* (Weidenfeld & Nicolson, London: 1986), Harold Nicolson, *King George V: His Life and Reign* (Macmillan, London: 1958 (also Nigel Nicolson (ed), Harold Nicolson, *Diaries and Letters 1930–1939* [Collins, London: 1966]), David Marquand, *Ramsay MacDonald* (Jonathan Cape, London: 1977), Keith Middlemas (ed), *Thomas Jones Whitehall Diary Vol I 1916–1925* (Oxford University Press, London: 1969), and Keith Middlemas (ed), *Thomas Jones' Whitehall Diary Vol II 1926–1930* (Oxford University Press, London: 1969), Norman and Jeanne Mackenzie (eds), *The Diary of Beatrice Webb, vol III 1905–24* and *vol IV 1924–1943* (Virago, London: 1984, 1985) and Robert Skidelsky, *John Maynard Keynes, The Economist as Saviour 1920–1937* (Macmillan, London: 1992), and HRH The Duke of Windsor, *A King's Story* (Cassell, London: 1951).

PICTURE SOURCES

Pages 60–1
In a safer age, an unaccompanied Stanley Baldwin walks across Whitehall towards Parliament, circa 1935. (Courtesy akg Images)

Pages 108–9
Stanley and Lucy Baldwin photographed in Brookville, Canada. They were among the retinue accompanying Edward, Prince of Wales on a tour of the Dominion in 1932. (Courtesy Topham Picturepoint)

Page 123
Among the first of the pipe-smoking premiers, Stanley Baldwin lights up, circa 1934.
(Courtesy Topham Picturepoint)

INDEX

A

Amery, Leo 40
Asquith, Herbert Henry 13,
    41, 42, 43, 68
Attlee, Clement 119

B

Baldwin, Alfred (father) 2,
    5, 6, 9, 85
Baldwin, Harold 4
Baldwin, Lucy (wife) 6, 7,
    13, 14, 21, 23, 24, 55,
    79, 121, 122
Baldwin, Oliver (son) 7, 13,
    34, 70, 89, 128
Beaverbrook, Lord 22, 28,
    70 ff., 72, 112, 116 ff.,
    118, 122
Bevin, Ernest 133
Bonar Law, Andrew 13, 18,
    21, 22 ff., 25, 26, 27, 29,
    31, 32, 33, 39
Boyce, John 7, 128
Broome, Phyllis 7
Bruce, Stanley 115
Burne-Jones, Sir Edward 3
Burrows, Arthur 131
Butler, Rab 91, 132

C

Campbell, J R 44
Chamberlain, Austen 9 ff.,
    14, 18, 20, 22, 31, 33,
    34, 37, 40, 43, 103
Chamberlain, Joseph 10,
    40, 85
Chamberlain, Neville 41,
    42, 48, 64, 67, 71, 72,
    74, 78, 79, 81, 85, 86,
    87, 97, 114, 120, 121,
    122, 127, 134, 137, 140
Churchill, Winston 10, 15,
    42, 47, 48, 50, 51, 52,
    57, 58, 64, 67, 72, 74,
    91 ff., 95, 96, 98, 103,
    105, 106, 116, 117, 118,
    120, 122, 136, 137, 138
    ff., 140 ff.
Citrine, Walter 132, 133
Clynes, J R 17
Cook, Arthur 57
Cooper, Duff 69, 74, 75
Cowling, Maurice 19, 23, 34
Crozier, W P 88
Cunliffe-Lister, Philip (Lord
    Swinton) 81, 98
Cunningham, William 8

Curzon, Lord 20, 23, 25, 27, 31, 37, 40, 41, 42, 47, 115

D

Davidson, J C C 22, 32, 42, 71, 72, 78, 84, 98, 130
Davidson, Joan 7
Davidson, Mimi 63
Dawes, General 38
Dawson, Geoffrey 64, 79, 80, 82, 89, 121
Dawson, Lord 110
Derby, Lord 34, 39, 73, 84
Disraeli, Benjamin 1, 2, 7, 127

E

Eden, Anthony 98, 103, 104, 105, 121, 140
Edward VIII, King 111 ff., 115 ff.

F

Feiling, Keith 127
Fisher, Sir Warren 94, 95
Foot, Michael 122
Furness, Lady 112

G

George V, King 31, 32, 41, 42, 44, 56, 57, 68, 79 ff., 110 ff., 115

George VI, King 119, 121
Griffith-Boscawen, Arthur 22

H

Hague, William 47
Hailsham, Lord 67
Hankey, Sir Maurice 94
Hardinge, Sir Alex 112, 113, 116
Henderson, Arthur 17
Hitler, Adolf 17, 76, 91, 94, 95 ff., 97, 104, 107, 120
Hoare, Samuel 81, 98, 101, 102, 119
Horne, Sir Robert 14, 34, 38

I

Inskip, Sir Thomas 104

J

Jenkins, Roy 33, 34, 41, 57 ff., 76
Jones, Tom 89, 95, 100
Joynson-Hicks, Sir William 10, 48, 53, 65, 66 ff.

K

Kelmsley, Lord 113
Keynes, John Maynard 19, 35, 52, 84

Kipling, John 13
Kipling, Rudyard 2, 47,
    110

L
Laval, Pierre 98, 101, 102
Leonard, Dick 131
Lindemann, Frederick 98
Lloyd George, David 13,
    15, 18, 19, 21, 22 ff., 24,
    34, 40, 41, 42, 51, 58,
    59, 65, 68, 69, 78, 83,
    86, 92, 97, 127, 134
Loch Mowat, Charles 66
Lockwood Kipling, John 4
Londonderry, Lady 59
Low, David 101

M
MacDonald, Louisa
    (mother) 2
MacDonald, Ramsay 17,
    43, 44, 46, 49, 68, 69,
    73, 77, 78, 79, 80, 81,
    82 ff., 86 ff., 88 ff., 93,
    94, 97, 126, 131, 136
Maclean, Sir Donald 85
Macmillan, Harold 69
Macquisten, David 49
Marlborough, Duke of 120
Marx, Karl 1
Mary, Queen 116
Maxton, Jimmy 17

May, Sir George 77
McKenna, Reginald 23, 38,
    41
McLean, Sir Donald 34
Monckton, Walter 116
Mond, Sir Alfred 54, 59
Morrison, Herbert 87
Mosley, Oswald 134
Mussolini, Benito 17, 98,
    101, 103

N
Nicolson, Harold 98, 106,
    113 ff., 119
Norfolk, Duke of 113
Norman, Montagu 26, 48,
    82

P
Poincaré, Raymond 38
Poynter, Ambrose 5
Poynter, Sir Edward 3

R
Reith, Lord John 122
Roosevelt, Franklin D 86,
    137
Rothermere, Lord 71, 72,
    112, 116
Runciman, Sir Walter 85

S
Salisbury, Lord 34, 88

Samuel, Sir Herbert 53, 56, 78, 79, 80, 82, 85
Scott, Sir Walter 3
Selassie, Haile 99, 103
Simon, Sir John 70, 71, 74, 83, 96, 97, 98
Simpson, Wallis 112 ff., 115 ff.
Sinclair, Sir Archibald 85
Skidelsky, Robert 85
Smith, F E (Lord Birkenhead) 18, 20, 34, 39, 40, 42, 47
Smith, Herbert 57
Snowden, Philip 77, 78, 86
Stalin, Josef 104, 137
Stamfordham, Lord 44

T

Taylor, A J P 136
Taylor, Andrew 21
Thatcher, Margaret 132
Thomas, Jimmy 110
Toynbee, Arnold 8

V

Vansittart, Robert 101, 103
Victoria, Queen 1

W

Webb, Mary 3
Webb, Sydney 17, 79
Wheatley, John 43
Wigram, Clive 110
Wilkinson, Ellen 87
Williamson, Philip 7
Wood, Edward (Lord Irwin, Viscount Halifax) 67, 70
Worthington-Evans, Sir Lamming 38

Y

York, Duke of 116
Young, G M 5, 33, 39,73, 122
Younger, Sir George 18, 24

Z

Zinoviev, Gregory 46, 136